"I'm someone who loves the outdoors but truly sucks at actually being in the wilderness. Chris has thought of every single thing you need to cook amazing food outside, and how to make it easy. *Cook It Wild* showed me I can enjoy our incredible planet and still have a killer meal at the end of the day."
– Matty Matheson, chef, actor, and author of *Matty Matheson: Home Style Cookery*

"If you like to camp, this exuberant book will change your life. Even if you don't, it's filled with terrific do-ahead dishes and smart kitchen tips that will make your life much easier."
—Ruth Reichl, author of *Save Me the Plums*

"I adore this book for at least two hundred reasons. Here are my top three: First, *Cook It Wild* is packed (pun intended) with the exact info you need to make every meal a delicious wilderness adventure. Second, Chris Nuttall-Smith is the definition of a "pro"—a stellar cook and an equally accomplished outdoorsman. I would trust him implicitly, with my dinner and my life. And third, with *Cook It Wild,* there's no excuse for mediocre meals. It's a campfire game changer."
—Gail Simmons, food expert, TV host, and author of *Bringing It Home*

"*Cook it* ideas. Th like a gro how not to just survive in the wild, but *thrive* indulgently—and that's before you get to a single mouthwatering recipe! (Of which there are many.) Roughing it has never looked so polished."
—David Zilber, chef, *New York Times* bestselling coauthor of *The Noma Guide to Fermentation*

"Chris actually makes me feel like I can camp! That I can conquer the outdoors and honestly, like I can conquer anything. Chris's tips and tricks to prepare for outdoor living are fantastic. Not only does he cover must-haves but makes it sound reasonable, approachable, and so incredibly tasty!"
—Eden Grinshpan, television host and author of *Eating Out Loud*

"I never thought I'd say, 'I need to go camping!' but that's all I can think after reading Chris Nuttall-Smith's fantastic new book. It's smart, it's insightful, and it makes me want to cook outdoors. Chris has convinced me that his recipes are actually going to taste even more delicious eaten around a campfire."
—Amanda Cohen, chef and owner of Dirt Candy

COOK IT WILD

Long-Haul Red
Lentil Dal, p.116

Sensational Prep-Ahead Meals for Camping, Cabins, and the Great Outdoors

COOK IT WILD

CHRIS NUTTALL-SMITH

PHOTOGRAPHS BY MAYA VISNYEI
ILLUSTRATIONS BY CLAIRE MCCRACKEN

CLARKSON POTTER/PUBLISHERS
NEW YORK

For Carol and Cormac, the greatest
campmates a guy could hope for. And for my
dad, who taught me how to write—and to never,
ever pitch a tent below the tide line.

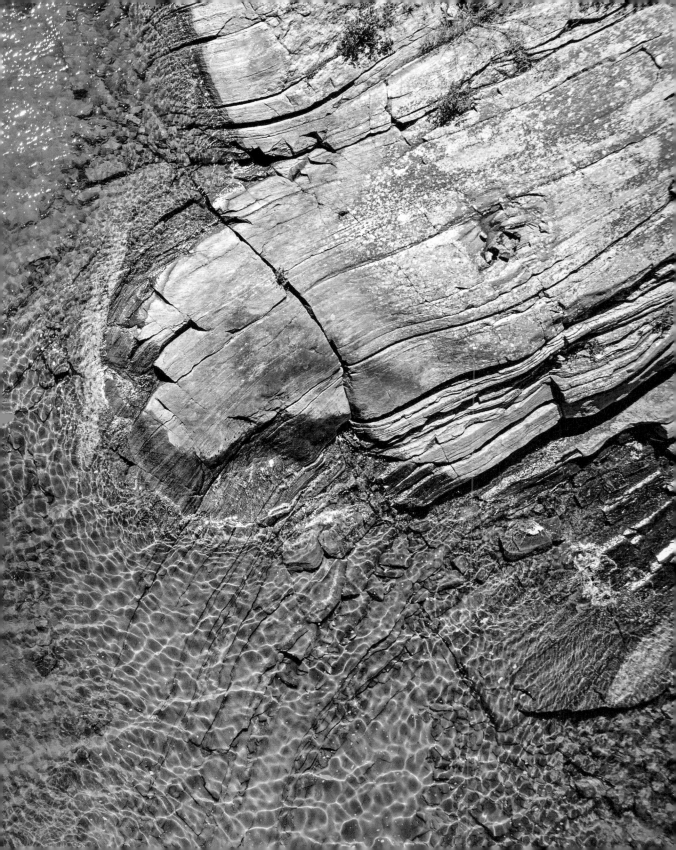

Contents

Introduction

The trip began with a big misunderstanding. I'd invited a group of friends for a weekend of wilderness camping, a two-hour paddle into a postcard of a park where we'd have a remote northern lake all to ourselves. The water, I promised, would be warm and calm and as clear as gin. The scenery would take their breath away. There'd be crackling campfires, raucous games of Cheat, and hammocks swaying in the summer breeze. And we would eat and drink like, well—this was camping, I warned them. There were no fridges, or food delivery, or dishwashers for the cleanup. We'd have a single backpacking burner as our stove. Plus, we'd have to pack light. So, of course, my friend Sasha shows up with a block of frozen squid.

As she told me what she had planned for the menu, I listened with growing alarm. There would be buttery roasted meats and vegetables, fire-baked flatbreads, platters of drinking snacks, and "a showstopper," as she called it, for Sunday night. It all sounded great, but I had no idea how she'd pull it off. We hadn't come out here to sweat over dinner all day.

The others in the group got the same memo: "Pack light" is apparently camping code for "bring the entire contents of your fridge." They planned buttermilk pancakes, freshly baked biscuits, fried lake-fish sandwiches, and fancy cocktails for twenty. (We were a party of nine.) What they didn't bring was freeze-dried, canned, or instant anything. Or as most people would call it, *camping food*.

Part of me understood their enthusiasm, at least. When I wasn't paddling northern lake chains with food-obsessed friends or backpacking Rocky Mountain passes, I earned my living as a food writer, well-traveled restaurant critic, and a judge on TV cooking shows. But until that weekend, I'd always kept my outdoor and food lives separate. I assumed that wild living and really good eating just didn't mix. Yet what happened through the next forty-eight hours wasn't the fiasco I expected. Although they were short on experience at cooking in the wild, each of them was a fanatical meal prepper. They'd done the work *in advance*.

When we finally pulled in to our lakeside site, those friends of mine set to pouring drinks that they'd mixed and frozen ahead. They served fresh lime margaritas and slushy white wine. Frosty negronis tasted sweet and bitter and magnificently boozy, and they hit with a brain-freezing jolt. A plate of country ham appeared, along with sliced summer sausage and fat, sweet cherries; then lacy, crunchy, creamy cacio e pepe–style flapjacks—what Italians call *farinata*—from a just-add-water batter that could last months on end in a pack.

We had more standout meals through that single weekend than I'd eaten in a lifetime outdoors. But what stuck out the most was how ingeniously effortless it all was. If it could be chopped, measured, mixed, marinated, braised, frozen, or fully premade at home, my friends had done it ahead. And meal prepping for the wild doesn't have to mean endless at-home kitchen labor, either. I began to see simple, practical, high-reward hacks that could dramatically change the way we cooked and ate outside.

"Prep ahead" could mean melty, sublimely tender, fire-roasted vegetables that took five minutes of hands-on time at home. Or instant, make-anywhere (as in make-it-at-7,500-feet-behind-a-windbreak-as-a-storm-rolls-in *anywhere*) shallot and cheese fondue that'd blow minds pretty much any place on Earth. It could mean comforting, protein-packed, no-refrigeration curries and killer Japanese-style slaw on Day 7 of a trip, just when the crunchy vegetable daydreams were starting to get intense.

Just ten minutes of dumping dry ingredients into a bag at home could mean moist, exquisite chocolate-chunk fire cake from a simple mix—zero eggs required.

And yeah, I guess you could even eat *squid* while camping. My friend Sasha's absurd-seeming packing soon started to make perfect(ish) sense.

On our second night at that lakeside campsite, Sasha seared it over the fire with pre-caramelized vegetables and Spanish rice, turning what I had been sure was the all-time dumbest-ever camping protein into the star of a smoky, spicy, spectacularly crackly crusted paella. I'm pretty sure it was the greatest thing I ate all year. (You'll find the recipe on page 131.)

We were stuffing our faces in the starlight one night when someone mumbled, "This is camping?" All I could think was that everyone should be eating this well outside.

Cook It Wild isn't just another camping cookbook. By harnessing the hassle-free power of meal prepping, *Cook It Wild* puts sensational outdoor eating in the hands of any camper or cook. Many of its very best recipes take little more effort in the wild than tipping fully prepped ingredients into a pot, onto a platter, or over the coals in the wild. More than half of the recipes in *Cook It Wild* take ten minutes or less at camp.

With its practical advice on planning, prepping, and packing for your trip, this book will vastly expand what you think of as "camping food" too. Because isn't it time that camp cooking caught up with how people actually want to eat? *Cook It Wild* offers softly caramelized sumac-roasted shallots and breathtakingly tasty dan dan noodles. It's simple, pre-prepped flatbreads that turn blistered and smoky over a camp stove or fire. Lightweight, one-pot red lentil dal that can be packed for roughing it but tastes every bit like glamping, and takes about as long to serve as reconstituting a freeze-dried meal. There's even a sublimely creamy risotto, real whipped cream (zero whisking required!), and the best near-instant French toast you'll ever eat.

Better still, *Cook It Wild* is designed with *your* wild in mind, no matter how or where you like to get outside. Whether you're a backpacker, a car or RV camper, a beach rat (hands up!), or a paddler. Whether your wild place of choice is a ski hut, cabin, hunting or fishing camp or cottage, the local park, or a cozy backyard, we have you covered.

This book's seventy-five-plus field-tested recipes are categorized with simple symbols so you can tell, at a glance, the types of trips they're ideal for, what special gear they may require, and even how much they'll weigh in your pack. Also, since pretty much nobody wants to bring a cookbook camping, *Cook It Wild* is designed so you can leave it at home: Every recipe's "At Camp" instructions are laid out so you can easily snap a photo to carry on the device of your choice.

But most important of all, *Cook It Wild* keeps front and center *why* we camp. We do it to get away, to recharge, and to spend quality time with friends and family. We do all this because it's ridiculous and, yes, *delicious* fun—and you can absolutely do it too.

AT-HOME BASICS

It all starts at your kitchen counter.

Here's how to plan for incredible outdoor eating, what to pack, and how to pack it, whether you're headed to the mountains for a five-day trek, or car camping with the kids for a night. Plus, the five simple keys to meal-prepping for the wild.

The Five Keys

Cook It Wild's empowering make-ahead, prep-ahead system is built around just five simple keys: Chop Ahead, Mix Ahead, Cook Ahead, Seal Ahead, and Freeze Ahead.

Some of the recipes incorporate every one of these, while others may use just one or two. But together, they unlock delicious, accessible, trip-making eating. Embrace them in your at-home prep, and you'll never look at camping food the same.

CHOP AHEAD

Anything you can chop, mince, trim, grate, grind, food-process, puree, or otherwise break down in advance without a loss of quality, you should. It saves time and effort when you're out in the wild, and it makes most foods smaller and lighter to pack.

By cutting up vegetables at home, you can bring exactly the quantity your recipes need while leaving seeds, cores, and peels behind. By trimming meats of unwanted fat, skin, and bones, you'll have far less at-camp trash.

You'll also need less kitchen gear in the wild, make less mess, and cook more quickly and efficiently.

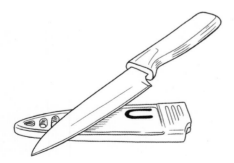

MIX AHEAD

Anything that can be mixed ahead, should. That means spice blends for grilling, dry mixes for biscuits and pancakes, and doughs for flatbreads and baked desserts. Premix salad dressings before you leave, and marinate proteins ahead of your trip.

Need grated cheese and butter at camp to finish a pasta? Combine them at home into a compound butter. A sauce for noodles or spiced honey for cheese? They're done before you ever roll up to your site.

The mix-ahead rule saves space, time, and at-camp effort. And it dramatically minimizes the packaging and containers you'll need to bring into the wild.

COOK AHEAD

Why caramelize shallots or onions at camp—using fuel and taking up time—when you can do it ahead and they're every bit as good? Why wait until you're tired (in a good way) and starving (all that fresh air!) to cook down a curry paste for an easy bowl of quick-cooking legumes (see page 116)?

Cooking ahead applies to showstopper lemon ribs (see page 138), which get braised at home, so they're fall-apart tender and loaded with flavor before you ever put them on the grill. Ground pork and cubed tofu get seasoned and oven-dehydrated weeks in advance; that pack-stable tofu will star in your instant ramen dreams (see page 207). Hardy greens, like collards and spinach, cook beautifully ahead of time, and the same goes for soft vegetables such as green beans.

Cooking ahead helps keep food from spoiling and decreases its packed weight by cooking off its water. It even makes many camp foods tastier, like shallot-y baked beans (see page 120) and rosemary butter nuts (see page 54), which are always more delicious a few days after they're made.

SEAL AHEAD

Wrap, pack, and seal whatever you can to optimize your food's lifespan, simplicity, and deliciousness.

Sealing ahead means repacking condiments and sauces into light, reusable containers so you don't have to bring the entire jar. Wrap tender greens, soft fruits, and vegetables smartly (see "Of Course You Can Bring Eggs!" on page 15), so they last for days on end.

Prep and fill foil vegetable packets (see page 95) while you're still at home, so you can slide them straight onto the grill.

For cheeses, sealing ahead often means *un*sealing them—removing them from the plastic wrap they came in and placing them in breathable parchment paper instead. (See "The Best Cheeses to Bring" on page 17.) For wine and spirits, transfer them from heavy, fragile glass into lighter, stronger containers—which also makes freezing them ahead easier. (See "The Art of the Seal" on page 14.)

FREEZE AHEAD

Whatever can be frozen ahead without a loss of taste or texture should be. Freezing food and beverages can dramatically extend their useful life. (Look for the ❄ symbol throughout *Cook It Wild*'s at-camp ingredient lists.)

Freezing ahead means you can prep showstopper Sizzling Cumin Lamb Kebabs (page 144) well before your trip. Pack cooked black beans or chickpeas without the cans, and eat crumbled feta cheese on Day 4 of your trip—without taking along its heavy brine. Freezing ahead turns rigatoni with Sunday meat sauce (see page 106) into dead-easy camping food. Enjoy fast food–style shrimp burgers (see page 186) in the middle of nowhere with lemony, deliciously sugary Dutch babies (see page 227) for dessert. Plus, slushy cocktails, fresh-tasting salsas, and pre-marinated meats. And a bonus: Everything you freeze helps cool the rest of your food.

Always be sure when freezing liquids to leave a bit of headspace in the bottle; the liquid will expand as its temperature drops. And suck or squeeze the air from resealable bags before sealing them for freezing. This will help protect your food from freezer burn.

The Art of the Seal

For condiments, sauces, oils, prepared batters, pickles, syrup, salt, sugar, and myriad other foodstuffs, Nalgene's reusable jars and bottles are easy to find, affordable, and effectively indestructible. Note that the jars are best for dry goods, though; anything liquid and leak-prone is best left to the bottles.

Alternatively, silicone food tubes are increasingly popular, although they generally don't come cheap.

Resealable bags, whether silicone zip-tops or otherwise, are indispensable for carrying snacks, cereals, and other ingredients, as well as for protecting prep-ahead vegetables and sauces from freezer burn. No matter what kind of bag you use, be sure to press or suck the air out of it before sealing. Your food will last longer that way.

Although strictly optional for *Cook It Wild*'s recipes, vacuum sealers and their bags protect food from freezer burn and extend the pack and cooler life of almost any meal. If you have a sealer, you can use it anywhere that calls for a resealable bag, bearing in mind that vacuum bags are not generally resealable out in the field.

For beverage-specific packing advice, see "The 7 Habits of Highly Effective Wild Drinkers," page 79.

Of Course You Can Bring Eggs!

(How to Pack the Delicate Stuff)

Eggs may take a bit of care, but they aren't nearly as hard to pack as you'd think. If you plan to scramble, make an omelet, or otherwise use them beaten at camp, whisk at home and then freeze the raw mixture in a leakproof container. Keep them cold and eat within two days of thawing.

For whole eggs, forget those yellow plastic egg carriers—unless you're into getting broken egg all over your stuff. Instead, cut a standard cardboard egg-carton to whatever size you need, then double-wrap it with a second carton. Tape the package shut and stick it in a resealable bag. (See the note about washed versus unwashed eggs on page 158.)

Tender herbs, like cilantro, parsley, thyme, rosemary, and sage, hold up well in cool to moderate temperatures, provided you wrap them first. Trim away any brown stems and be sure to discard any pieces that are slimy, wilted, or not perfectly fresh. Wash the herbs in cold water, then dry them in a salad spinner or on a clean kitchen towel. Lay a length of paper towel on your counter, then place the herbs on it so they're ½ inch apart. (It's important that they're not touching.) Now roll up the paper towel from one end to the other, enveloping the herbs inside it as you roll. Label the roll and store it in a bag left open at the top for ventilation. Avoid crushing the whole thing if you can.

This paper towel–rolling method works great for delicate vegetables such as miniature cucumbers, greens such as endive and radicchio, tender vegetables such as green onions and baby lettuces, and even cooked undressed string beans. Keep them all cool.

The best-tasting tomatoes are heavy, prone to bruising, don't do well in coolers (the cold can turn their flavor insipid), and make a sticky mess when they aren't handled with care. Yet, it's hard to imagine camping without at least a few of them. The vented clamshell containers many hothouse varieties come in do a terrific job of protecting them, as do reusable plastic food containers. Baby them like the wilderness gold they are.

Soft summer fruit, whether they're peaches, plums, nectarines, or super-tender berries, travel reasonably well in the pint containers they're sold in, as well as in the larger cardboard baskets many fruit stands still use. If you're backpacking, that's going to be a stretch; but in a tripping canoe or on the dashboard of a camper van, it's a medium-effort/high-reward proposition. Buy stone fruit and strawberries a bit unripe; it doesn't take long for them to soften up in the sun. Line the containers with a sheet of paper towel (to soak up moisture), and make sure to keep the berries ventilated—they'll turn in no time if it's warm and they can't breathe.

The Right Dairy for Any Kind of Trip

Being in the wild doesn't have to mean giving up milk, cream, nut milks, and other nondairy alternatives. Here's a rundown of the options and how to use them.

DRY MILK

The lightest, most pack-stable, and most time-tested choice.

Instant milk powder is the most widely used dry dairy product, especially in the outdoors. Simply mix it with water to make liquid milk, or sprinkle it over food or into hot drinks for milky, creamy flavor and texture. (See the sugared oatmeal topper on page 175.) Although non-fat and skim versions are typically the easiest to find, whole and low-fat instant milks are also available. Be sure to check for the word "instant" when purchasing dry milk; non-instant varieties, although excellent for baking, are harder to mix and often have a cooked taste reminiscent of evaporated milk.

Powdered buttermilk is brilliant in pancakes, biscuits, and other baked goods. It adds dairy tang, tenderness, and light airy leavening. Find it in well-stocked baking sections of supermarkets, in bulk stores, or online.

Powdered coconut milk and powdered coconut cream are inexpensive, shelf-stable, calorie-dense (great for backpackers!), and easy to mix. They're surprisingly tasty, too, with a full, creamy texture and flavor that's not far from fresh. Try them sprinkled on hot or cold cereal, added to the water when cooking rice, or poured over dessert.

Powdered soy milk, cashew milk, oat milk, and even goat milk powders, are also increasingly available in health food stores and online.

UHT

Ultra-high temperature (UHT) processed dairy is the everyday standard across Europe and much of the world, in large part because it's shelf-stable until opened. Although less popular in North America, UHT milk is nonetheless widely available—and perfect for camping. You can find it at major retailers as well as online.

UHT whipping cream can be harder to find— Trader Joe's has been one of the main sources. When available, the 8-ounce cartons are perfect for drizzling over campfire desserts.

And UHT soy, rice, oat, and nut milks are pretty much everywhere, including in pack-friendly juice-box formats.

FRESH MILK

Not much tastes better than the real thing, especially on short-duration and cooler-equipped trips. If you'd rather freeze them, cream and milk both benefit from a vigorous post-thaw shaking.

CANNED MILK

Canned evaporated milk is heat-treated to remove more than half of its water. It's good in hot drinks or reconstituted 1:1 with water, but has a notably caramelized taste.

Sweetened condensed milk is essentially evaporated milk, but with a whole lot of sweetener added. It's a traditional component of Vietnamese coffee and many desserts. (See the Buttered-Rum Coffee Cake on page 228.)

The Best Cheeses to Bring

(and How to Keep Them from Going All Sweaty)

If you'll have a fridge or ice wherever you're headed, bring whatever you love. But if you need a few good cheeses that will last when unrefrigerated (see Note), here are some standouts. Just be sure to wrap them as directed.

Hard and aged cheeses will always pack best for longer trips or spotty refrigeration.

Parmigiano-Reggiano and Grana Padano last weeks in a pack if you don't let them get hot.

Aged sheep's milk Pecorino cheeses are similarly durable; they bring a savory punch reminiscent of the Parms, but with a deliciously salty, briny, grassy edge. Pecorino Romano is brilliant for grating over pastas and is also the hero of cacio e pepe (see page 62).

Aged Manchego, from Spain, keeps nicely unrefrigerated, while most aged Gouda-style cheeses, including ever-popular Beemster, arguably taste better when stored unrefrigerated. Aged cheddar can go weeks without refrigeration too.

Many French cheeses are traditionally stored unrefrigerated. The bright-orange, caramel-tasting Mimolette keeps beautifully, as does aged Gruyère (the backbone of the shallot-cheese fondue on page 201) and mild, buttery Comté. And small, rind-covered goat cheeses, like Chabichou and Charolais—think of the little gray pyramids and pucks you might have seen at the cheese counter—are often stars in a backpack. Be sure they're dry and firm to the touch when you buy them, and if they start to get soft or oozy, that's your cue to finish them up.

Even firm blue cheeses such as English Stilton and Spanish Valdeón are remarkably hardy when unrefrigerated.

And although caseophiles might be pained to hear this, those processed, foil-wrapped The Laughing Cow triangles are shelf-stable for weeks, if not months. As are wax-wrapped Babybel cheeses; my kid has basically lived on them through extended wilderness trips.

HOW TO WRAP CHEESE

Whether you've got a fridge, cooler or otherwise, your cheese will last longer and taste better if you wrap it right. The best scenario for storage is usually vacuum-packed; if it came that way from your cheesemonger, leave it vac-packed until you're ready to dig in. But once it's opened, the most important thing is to let it breathe to prevent off-flavors and mold.

FOR CHEESES THAT WILL BE KEPT COLD

Wrap your cheese in a sheet of parchment paper, followed by aluminum foil. The parchment lets it breathe; the foil keeps it from drying out. Label using a Sharpie and you're good to go.

WRAPPING FOR UNREFRIGERATED STORAGE

Wrap the cheese in a layer or two of clean, cotton cheesecloth, then wrap it again in aluminum foil. The fabric will absorb and retain the butterfat droplets—aka cheese sweat—that separate out; this helps keep it moist *and* schvitz-free.

Note

→ "Unrefrigerated" here means 70°F or cooler; hot temperatures will shorten the life of most cheese.

How to Pack a Cooler

START COLD

Coolers are best at *keeping* things cold—not at making them that way. Everything that goes in should be cold from the start. Freeze any foods or liquids that can be frozen ahead (see page 13). Anything else should go in straight from the fridge.

And the "start cold" rule applies to the actual cooler too. If you store it in a warm place, chill it down with water or sacrificial ice, then drain it before you pack.

USE ENOUGH ICE

For long-lasting cold, aim for a ratio of 2:1—two parts ice for every one part food or drink. If that seems like *a lot* of ice, remember: All that food and drink you froze ahead counts toward the total.

WHAT KIND OF ICE?

Block ice—sold alongside bags of the cubed stuff—is the best for the bottom of your cooler. (It's also easy to make; see following.) Cubes are best for filling air gaps once the cooler's full (air gaps warm coolers fast). For larger coolers, I'm a fan of reusable Techni Ice sheets for the gap between the food and the underside of the lid.

If you have the freezer space at home, consider making your own ice blocks in repurposed cartons, jugs, or water bottles. Or do what Grand Canyon river guides do: Fill the bottom of a hard cooler with 4 to 5 inches of water and stick it in a large freezer (with the cooler lid open!) 'til everything's solid.

And remember: Not all ice is created equal. Always start with hard, frosty ice; it'll last longer than ice that's wet or soft.

MELTWATER IS YOUR FRIEND

That melty water sloshing at the bottom of your cooler serves an important purpose: It takes up space that warm air would otherwise fill. And as long as the water has some ice left in it, it's plenty cold enough to keep your food chilled.

BUT KEEP FOOD AND MELTWATER SEPARATE

Resealable, watertight bags or stackable food containers will keep your food protected from a cooler's meltwater. As a bonus: They help keep your cooler organized, which means you'll spend less time rooting around for things.

SHUT THE FREAKING LID!

The less you open your cooler, the longer it'll stay cold. Transfer high-frequency grabs—drinks, especially—to a smaller cooler if you have the space. And if you're traveling in a group, or bulk is not an issue, consider packing two coolers instead of one. One is dedicated to a trip's first day or two, and then becomes the drinks cooler; the second one doesn't get opened (not even a peep!) until later on.

THROW SOME SHADE

No matter how rugged or pricey a cooler you buy, it's no contest for direct sun or the heat of a scorching vehicle. Keep its exterior cool as best you can. If it's got to be in the sun, cover it with a foam sleeping pad, lifejackets, wet fabric (for evaporative cooling), or other items to keep the heat off.

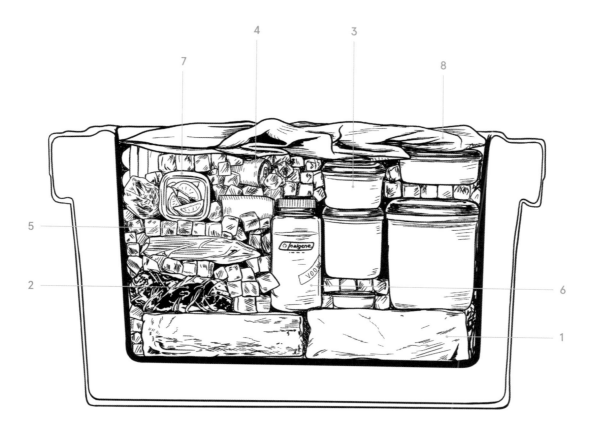

Modern heavy-duty, high-insulating coolers have dramatically changed what kinds of foods and drinks belong in the wild. But they don't mean a thing if you don't pack them right. Whether you're hauling a 5-quart soft-sider, a canoe-friendly 30-quart-er, or a bear-resistant, hard-sided, 120-quart behemoth, here's how to keep your deliciousness cold.

1. Place block ice at the bottom for long-lasting cold.

2. Set frozen and later-trip items directly on the ice. This is the coldest area in the cooler.

3. Use containers or resealable bags to organize your food and protect it from meltwater.

4. Place early-trip items near the top. No sense digging around for things you'll need right away.

5. Pour ice cubes into any air gaps.

6. Stand bottles and other tall items upright if your cooler allows it. They're easier to find that way.

7. Anything fragile or less perishable should go near the top.

8. Fill the air gap under the lid with a towel (good) or sheet ice (best).

My Condiments to the Chef

A well-curated selection of camp condiments can help make a meal. Here are a few gimmes.

CLASSIC

- → Ketchup, mustard, and relish packets
- → Olive oil
- → Plum sauce takeout packets
- → Soy sauce takeout packets
- → Vinegar packets

CREAMY

- → Hellmann's mayo packets
- → Olive tapenade
- → Tartar sauce

SWEET

- → Fig jam and Spanish membrillo (killer with cheese)
- → Maple syrup
- → Raw honey

SPICY

- → Bomba sauce
- → Calabrian peperoncini piccanti
- → Harissa paste in a tube
- → Horseradish root, fresh or prepared
- → Powdered hot mustard (Colman's every time)
- → Tabasco, sriracha, and sambal oelek packets
- → Wasabi in a tube

Packing Everything Else

The finer details of how people pack their food can get highly personal. Some campers pack a different food bag for each day of their trip. Others (including me) do four siliconized stuff sacks: one for breakfast ingredients; one for lunches; one for cocktail snacks and dinners; and one for desserts, trail snacks, and staple ingredients.

All that matters is finding a system that works for you. Preferably a system that's at least somewhat organized. (A basic meal list, combined with a little labeling, can go a very long way.) Because there's only one certainty that I've gleaned through the years: Throwing your food randomly into a single bag is closely correlated with frustrated cursing at mealtimes.

The Instant, Awesome, Easy-to-Find Eats That Belong in Every Pack

(for When You Can't Be Bothered)

I like to call these "emergency rations."

Boil-in-a-Bag Curry
The best are as good as takeout. The worst are still pretty good.

Boil-in-a-Bag Instant Rice
Quick, comforting, deliciously empty calories. Zero cleanup.

Chocolate Hazelnut and Almond Butter Packets
An ounce and a bit of instant happiness.

Fancy Chocolate
You've probably earned it.

Foil-Packed Fish
Tasty, tear-open protein for soups, starches, salads, and sandwiches.

Foil-Packed Olives
Gin and martini glasses optional.

Freeze-Dried Fruit
It's not another bag of banana chips.

Instant Korean Noodle Soup
What Mr. Noodles wishes he could be.

Instant Miso Soup Packets
Weighs nothing. Tastes delicious. A warm hug for your electrolytes.

Instant Risotto
Puts pretty much every freeze-dried backpacking entrée to shame. A slice of compound Reggiano butter (see page 110), if you have it, is the pro move here.

Jerky
Plenty of fancy butcher and charcuterie shops make top-shelf gourmet takes, but in a pinch, even the gas-station brands can be pretty good.

OvaEasy Egg Crystals
Dad-joke name, winning taste and texture. Whether in hashes, on chilaquiles, or smothered with hot sauce, you'd be hard-pressed to distinguish these from fresh eggs.

Roasted Seaweed
Caloric value? Negligible. But still.

Shelf-Stable Bacon
Ordinary bacon, but pre-cooked and vac-packed. Win-win.

Snickers Bars
You'd be shocked at the number of wilderness athletes who live on these things. Also? Tasty!

Sugary Processed Peanut Butter
For when you need your moody preteen (or hangry hiking partner) to go just one more &*%^$# mile.

Making a Plan

I have camping friends who can't leave home without minutely detailed meal, snack, and beverage spreadsheets. It works all right if you stay rigorously on-plan, don't mind the lectures (*You were supposed to eat the Funyuns on Day 2!*), and don't decide in a fit of, I don't know, *joy?* to eat an off-schedule cookie or two.

Other people I've camped with have no other plan than "bring way too much." They're convinced they're always just a few calories away from starvation.

But *Cook It Wild*'s trip type and gear symbols, plus its planning features, make planning your camp eating easy. Here's how.

TRIP TYPE

What kind of trip you're planning will have the biggest impact on what you pack, cook, and eat. (You can find a full run-down of *Cook It Wild*'s planning symbols on pages 48 and 49.)

For backpacking, bikepacking, ski touring, and other self-propelled travel, start at the recipes marked with the backpacking symbol. They're designed to be lightweight, reasonably long-lasting, and easy to prepare with minimal gear. And remember: The recommended trip types are guidelines only. If you're a backpacker, for instance, who prioritizes absurdly good eating, be sure to check out the recipes with paddling symbols too.

For paddling trips, you can typically pack along more weight and gear. A medium-size soft- or hard-sided cooler will also expand what food makes sense. Start your planning at the recipes marked with backpacking or paddling symbols before taking into consideration the other criteria listed.

For car camping, RVing, and cabin stays, you'll face the fewest limits. Any recipe with the backpacking, paddling, or car/RV symbols will work for your trip, subject to the other planning criteria listed.

To further fine-tune your food plan, every recipe includes its ingredient weight at the top, so you won't get a surprise when you sling on your pack.

You should also consider your group's expectations. Is it a destination trip, where you'll get to one spot and mostly hunker down? Or is your party's plan to be striking camp and setting up each day?

On most of the trips I do, it's a mix of the two, so I plan a combination of simple, delicious, quick-serve meals and leisurely, more involved ones. That mix also helps when it comes to prepping; a bit of what's simple and a bit of higher effort, so you're not knocking yourself out before you even leave.

And no matter how you're camping, here's a dose of reality: Not every meal you eat must be made from scratch. For those (all-important) times when you don't feel the cooking vibes, some well-chosen instant eats (see "The Instant, Awesome, Easy-to-Find Eats That Belong in Every Pack," page 20) are *exactly* the right choice.

TRIP LENGTH

The longer the trip, the more you'll need to bring. For self-propelled campers and paddlers especially, longer trips mean ingredient weight matters more, as do meals that can last without coolers and ice. So, dishes with ingredients that need to be kept cold are marked with the cooler symbol. And every recipe includes a breakdown of how long it keeps, so you'll know what makes sense for the later stages of a trip.

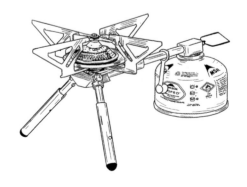

PARTY SIZE

Your group size not only determines how much food you'll need, but it changes what gear you can bring and how adventurous (or otherwise!) the eating and drinking should be. In group situations, it's easier to share that load of heavier gear. A cast-aluminum Dutch oven that would feel ridiculous for a solo camper or duo suddenly makes total sense for a party of six. (Hello, lemony, sugary Dutch babies!) And if there's more than one cook in your group, the eating can be more ambitious as you divide and conquer.

GEAR REQUIREMENTS

Will most of your cooking be done on a backpacking stove? Or do you plan to also cook over a fire? Will you be bringing a grill or a Dutch oven? Check the simple gear symbols, included with each recipe, to know what you'll need.

OTHER CONSIDERATIONS

The weather will impact what you can cook, what you can bring, and what you'll want to eat, so keep an eye on the forecast. High altitude can change how long it takes to cook many foods, how much fuel you'll need, and even how some recipes should be prepped ahead. (See "Cooking While High," page 122.)

It's important to call ahead or look up the regulations wherever you're headed—especially if it's your first time there. Many public areas prohibit fires in drought conditions; they're also forbidden in some environmentally fragile wilderness and alpine areas. Some parks don't allow glass bottles or any type of can, so you'll need to repack beverages and any canned goods before you leave home.

And critter-related requirements—the mandatory use of bear canisters or lockers, for example—are common in parks and wilderness areas across the continent. Look them up in advance so you'll know what you can bring.

CALORIES, PROTEIN, AND HOW MUCH YOU'LL NEED

For leisurely trips without much exertion, you already know what you need—it's how much you eat on any other sedentary day. That usually totals between 13.5 and 15 calories and up to 0.5 grams of protein per pound you weigh.

For moderate-intensity days of paddling, reasonably light hiking, or similar activities, your calorie requirements will increase slightly to between 16 and 20 calories per 1 pound of body weight. Your protein requirements may also increase somewhat; an extra 10 percent should typically do.

On high-intensity days or when winter camping, your body burns through far more calories. You'll need between 21 and 30 calories and 0.55 to 0.9 grams of protein per 1 pound of body weight.

And if you'll be more than an easy walk from civilization, a bit of extra is never a bad idea. I usually stick a few lightweight, calorie-dense meals at the bottom of a food bag—enough to get through an extra day in a pinch.

AT-CAMP BASICS

You've planned the perfect menu. Now you'll need some camp-kitchen essentials and know-how to pull it off in the wild. Here are the basics of cooking, drinking, and eating at camp, from filtering water and washing dishes to bear-proofing your provisions and building the right fire. Plus, all the best gear to bring your wild-feasting dreams alive.

Backpacking

Gear Guide

What to pack for two to four backpackers (or bikepackers, or backcountry skiers) when weight and bulk matter, but you still want to eat very (very) well.

COOKING

Lightweight backpacking stove
Recommended: MSR WhisperLite Universal Stove (See "How to Pick a Stove for Good Cooking," page 32.)

All-weather stove fuel
Recommended: MSR IsoPro Fuel

Windscreen
Recommended: MSR Solid Heat Reflector with Windscreen

Fire starters (lighters, waterproof matches)

Lightweight pot
Features to Look For: Foldaway handle, strainer lid, large enough to boil 1 pound of pasta
Recommended: Sea to Summit Alpha Pot, 3.7 liter

Nonstick skillet, 8 or 10 inches
Features to Look For: Heavy-gauge bottom for even heating, foldaway handle
Tip: Nonstick cookware takes babying, but it's worth it for delicate foods, like pancakes and fish. Keep these out of the cooking fire. And always use non-scratching utensils.
Recommended: GSI Outdoors Bugaboo Frypan

Silicone tongs
Tip: Great for nonstick pans, but all-metal tongs work better for high-temp grilling.

Folding spatula
Features to Look For: Heatproof, sharp-edged for inserting underneath food
Recommended: GSI Outdoors Pivot Spatula

Light, large, flexible cutting board
Tip: It doubles as a serving platter.
Recommended: IKEA Finfördela

Small kitchen knife with blade cover
Features to Look For: Inexpensive, lightweight, replaceable

SERVING

Cutlery

Mugs
Features to Look For: Stacking, marked with volume measurements (they double as measuring cups)

Plates, bowls

STORING

Cloth beeswax food wrappers
Tip: These do double duty as super-lightweight serving platters.

Reusable water bottles

Siliconized dry sack (for carrying it all)

Small, soft-sided cooler
Features to Look For: Weight/size/insulation balance that's good for you
Recommended: Hydro Flask Insulated Lunch Bag, 5 liter

Small mesh bag
Tip: For quickly cooling drinks in water, see "The 7 Habits of Highly Effective Wild Drinkers," page 79.

CLEANING AND MISCELLANEOUS

Biodegradable concentrated soap

Dish scrubber
Recommended: MSR Alpine Dish Brush/Scraper

Dishwashing bin (optional)
Recommended: Sea to Summit Kitchen Sink, 5 liter

Hand sanitizer

Leakproof trash bag
Recommended: Sea to Summit Trash Dry Sack

Paracord, 50 feet (or more)
Features to Look For: Type III 7-strand 550 rating.
Nothing's better for camping.

Small, fine-mesh strainer (for filtering food scraps from dishwater)
Tip: You won't be needing the handle, so cut it off.

Small squeeze-type water filter
Recommended: Platypus QuickDraw Microfilter System

Water purification tablets
(See "How to Treat Water So It's Safe for Drinking," page 39.)

Also review "How to Keep Your Food Safe from Critters Large and Small," page 44, for bear-resistant food-storage options.

Paddling

Gear Guide

You've got a bit more space and can handle a little more weight. Here's a stellar canoe or kayak kitchen setup for two to four trippers. (Note: For items with an *, you'll find more details in the Backpacking Gear Guide on pages 26 and 27.)

COOKING

Lightweight backpacking stove*
Recommended: Snow Peak BiPod Stove

Compact, roll-up grill (optional)
Recommended: Wolf and Grizzly M1 Grill

All-weather stove fuel*

Windscreen*

Fire starters

Fire-resistant pot, 3 liters (or larger)
Features to Look For: A heavy base to distribute heat, fireproof or foldaway handle, stainless-steel construction

Pot gripper
Tip: For pulling pots out of fires and off grills.

Nonstick skillet, 10 inches*

Paella pan, 13 inches (optional)
Features to Look For: Carbon-steel construction, dimpled base, no extra coatings
Tip: Not just for paella! Lightweight, super-durable, and shockingly affordable ($20 to $30), plus it can't be beat for cooking over a fire. On camp or backpacking stoves, though, they're prone to hot spots.
Recommended: La Paella Carbon Steel Paella Pan

Hard-anodized aluminum Dutch oven, 10 inches (optional)
(See "Everything You Need to Know about Dutch Ovens," page 224.)

Dutch-oven stand (optional)
Recommended: GSI Outdoors Universal Dutch Oven Stand

Silicone tongs*

Metal tongs
Tip: For live-fire cooking and high-temp grilling.

Folding spatula*

Silicone spatula

Light, large, flexible cutting board*

Small kitchen knife with blade cover*

Instant-read thermometer (optional)
Recommended: Thermapen ONE

Vegetable peeler
Tip: Just as useful for shaving hard cheeses as for peeling stuff.

Travel espresso pump (optional)
(See "When Great Coffee Is the Only Option," page 162.)

SERVING

Mugs*

Plates, bowls

Folding utility and serving knife

Cloth beeswax food wrappers*

Cutlery
Tip: Sure, a spork is fine. But a fork and a spoon are *deluxe*.

STORING

Midsize cooler (soft- or hard-sided)
Features to Look For: Heavy-duty insulation, leakproof zippers, bear-resistant, buoyant
Tip: You do not need to buy the most expensive, most influencer-promoted brand to find the best.

Reusable water bottles

Water-storage bag

Small mesh bag*

Soft-sided lunch and drinks cooler*

Stuff sacks for storing it all

CLEANING AND MISCELLANEOUS

Fire-resistant gloves

Folding firewood saw or hatchet (optional)

Gravity water-filter system*

Leakproof trash bag*

Paracord, 50 feet (or more)*

Dish scrubber* and Dishwashing bin*
Recommended: Sea to Summit Kitchen Sink, 10 liter

A couple kitchen towels

Hand sanitizer and Biodegradable concentrated soap*

Small, fine-mesh strainer*

Also review "How to Keep Your Food Safe from Critters Large and Small," page 44, for bear-resistant food-storage options.

Car, RV, and Cabin Camping

Gear Guide

You won't have to lug it on your back or in a little boat, but a well-chosen camp kitchen—as opposed to just bringing *everything*—will help you cook and eat at your best. Though your gear requirements will depend on how you're camping, here's a terrific starting point for two to four campers. (Note: For items with an *, you'll find more details in the Backpacking and Paddling Gear Guides on pages 26–29.)

COOKING

Two-burner camp stove
(See "How to Pick a Stove for Good Cooking," page 32.)

Propane tank (5 pounds) and adapter hose

Fire starters

Pot gripper*

Fire-resistant pot, 3 liters (or larger*)

Nonstick skillet, 12 inches*

Paella pan, 10 to 13 inches (optional)*

Hard-anodized aluminum Dutch oven, 10 inches (optional)*

Dutch-oven stand (optional)*

Water kettle

Silicone tongs*

Metal tongs*

"Everything" spatula
Tip: Although it's officially called a "fish spatula," you'll use this restaurant-supply staple as a camp-kitchen multitool. It slips under stuck-on food, it's great for serving, and, with its sharp edge, it will even cut your sandwiches right in the pan.

Non-scratch pancake spatula

Vegetable peeler*

Instant-read thermometer*

Zester-grater
Recommended: Microplane Premium Classic Series Cheese Grater and Zesting Tool

Lightweight pepper mill

Light, large, flexible cutting board*

Compact, roll-up grill (optional)*

Collapsible pour-over coffee filter basket
Recommended: SOTO Helix Coffee Maker

Ridiculously nice coffee grinder (optional)
Recommended: VSSL Java

Coffee filters
(See "When Great Coffee Is the Only Option," page 164.)

SERVING

Enamelware plates, bowls, mugs, and platters

Cutlery (knives, forks, and spoons)
Recommended: TOAKS Titanium 3-Piece Cutlery Set

STORING

Cloth beeswax food wrappers*

Hard-sided, bear-resistant cooler*

Midsize cooler (soft- or hard-sided)*

CLEANING AND MISCELLANEOUS

Water-storage bag

Flat-pack camp sink*

Biodegradable concentrated soap*

Dish scrubber*

Dishcloths and kitchen towels

Hand sanitizer

Fine-mesh strainer (for filtering food scraps from dishwater)

Gravity water-filter system

Paracord, 50 feet (or more)*

Pop-up trash can
Tip: Don't forget a liner bag!

Folding firewood saw or hatchet (optional)

How to Pick a Stove for Good Cooking

(and Bring Enough Fuel!)

No single piece of gear has a greater impact on what you can cook in the wild than the stove you bring. The best of them are as good as your burners at home: They're efficient, powerful, and easy to control, from a gentle simmer to a blazing roar. Here's what you need to know.

CAMP STOVE OR BACKPACKING STOVE?

Camp stoves are ideal for group cooking, large pots and pans, and more complex meals. Nothing beats their stability and ease of use. They usually have two burners, simmer reliably, and feature built-in windscreens. Many ignite with the push of a button. They typically run on propane, liquid camping fuel, or butane canisters. The drawback of camp stoves is their size and weight—they're not generally made for slipping into a pack.

Backpacking stoves are single burners, designed for self-propelled adventuring. Some are good at boiling water fast, but not much else—they're just too hot for lower-temperature cooking. Others work great for bigger groups and more complex meals, with dependable simmering and heat control. Backpacking stoves run primarily on either liquid camping fuel or isobutane canisters. And true to name, most of them are light and portable.

WHAT KIND OF FUEL?

For camp stoves, propane canisters are the most popular choice. They're widely available and work dependably in most climates. Propane comes with real drawbacks, though. The 1-pound canisters most propane-fueled camp stoves use are bulky, heavy, and single-use only, and their cost can add up fast. Because they don't always recycle easily, they're also an enormous source of hazardous waste.

Far better: Buy a refillable 5-pound propane tank and adapter hose to replace the canisters. They usually pay for themselves in a season or less.

Butane stoves are excellent to cook over; they're popular even in nonwild settings, especially among caterers and chefs. They're typically available as a mid-size option—a single, powerful, and comparatively inexpensive burner that's smaller than many camp stoves, but larger than backpacking ones. In freezing temperatures, however, they're all but useless, and the selection of butane stoves (not to be confused with isobutane canister models) is limited. Butane fuel bottles can also be a challenge to find at times. Still, for car and RV campers with limited space or no need for more than one burner, butane can be an excellent option.

Although it comes with significant downsides, liquid fuel, also called "white gas," is the most versatile choice. It's easy to find and works dependably in freezing temperatures. Because liquid-fuel stoves use refillable tanks and bottles, they create less waste as well. Some models will even burn kerosene or unleaded gas in a pinch. On the downside, these stoves require priming, which means igniting a small amount of the fuel to heat the burner. That often translates into a blazing fireball. The fuel bottles need frequent pressurizing, too, to keep your stove burning; the pumping can be a pain. And the stoves are notoriously bad at simmering. With few exceptions—or a whole lot of fussing—you get either a blowtorch or a sputtering flame, and not much in between. Still, for expedition-worthy reliability in almost any condition, liquid fuel comes out on top.

Pressurized isobutane canisters, which combine a mix of isobutane and propane gas, are light, efficient, simple to use, and mess-free. Paired with the right stove, they're also superb for simmering and lower-temperature cooking. On the downside, the canisters can be tough to find in some parts of the world. Some canister brands also don't work well in freezing temperatures; it's important to buy winter-optimized fuel mixes if you plan to cook in the cold. (They'll be clearly marked.) And although they can be recycled (the process requires fully emptying them, then punching holes in their tops), it's not as straightforward as many would hope, and it depends on local recycling facilities. Still, for campers who don't want the weight or the bulk of a camp stove, isobutane-fueled backpacking stoves are usually the best choice.

WHAT OTHER FEATURES MATTER?

Once you've chosen your stove and fuel types, here's how to dial in the rest.

HEAT CONTROL

If you want to do more than boil stuff fast (and you do!), make sure to get a model that simmers well. Your stove's heat knob(s) should allow for precise, easy adjustments. Also, wide-diameter burners (versus narrow ones) will help you avoid hot spots; you'll be thankful when using skillets.

OUTPUT

Camp stoves come in a wide range of British thermal unit (BTU) outputs, from 10,000 on average to 30,000 in the most powerful units. If you're cooking vats of sauce or lobster boils for twenty people, you may, at some point, find a need for that much heat. For everybody else, 20,000 BTUs is nice to have, especially in windy campgrounds and for larger pots, but 10,000 BTUs will also get the job done.

STABILITY

Many isobutane backpacking burners attach directly to the top of fuel canisters. Then your full pot of whatever sits on top of that. On anything less than perfectly flat ground, you're asking for trouble, especially with larger or fuller pots. (I call these systems "leaning towers of third-degree burns.") If you use a vertical-canister stove, make sure it comes with added supports to keep it from tipping. Or far better, get a remote-canister model, in which the burner sits flat on the ground or table, and the fuel is connected remotely with a hose.

WINDSCREEN COMPATIBILITY

Even a moderate wind will suck heat from a stove. Windscreens are standard on most camp stoves, and they're compatible with most liquid-fuel backpacking stoves, as well as many remote-canister isobutane models. Important note: They aren't safe to use with many vertical-canister backpacking burners, as they trap heat around the fuel bottles, which can explode as a result.

How Much Fuel?

Bring too much gas and you're lugging extra weight. Too little and you're eating your meals cold. Assuming optimal conditions, here are some (very) rough starting points:

→ 1 ounce of isobutane will boil up to 1.8 liters of water

→ 1 ounce of camping gas will boil up to 1.3 liters of water

→ 1 pound of propane will boil up to 20 liters of water

But it's important to note how widely that all can vary, depending on the conditions and your stove. Suboptimal conditions (high wind, cold or freezing air and water temperature, forgetting to put the lid on the pot) can triple or quadruple your stove's fuel consumption. And some stoves perform better, while others perform significantly less efficiently.

To calculate your fuel needs more precisely, there are plenty of online formulas available, and some manufacturers, including MSR and Jetboil, post their stoves' fuel-efficiency figures online. You can also test it out at home using your stove, a liter of water, a stopwatch (to time how long the water takes to boil), and a digital scale (for weighing how much fuel the boiling took). Combine those figures with the number of "boils" you'll need on your trip for a starting point.

However, your best bet when starting out is to pack plenty of extra fuel. If you can, do the calculations for boils per trip (remember the dishwater! And the coffee and hot chocolate!) and then add plenty more. Keep a record of how much you used for your first few times out. Getting it right will be second nature in no time at all.

Make the Right Fire for Your Food and Use It Like a Pro

(Hint: It's not the same as your campfire!)

THE ZONES

The best cooking fires have three distinct zones.

THE BURNING ZONE: Where fresh logs are added. The burning zone produces new coals and is typically too hot for cooking food without charring.

THE COOKING ZONE: Consists mostly of glowing coals. The cooking zone is where most of the grilling happens, as well as the heating of pots and pans.

THE INDIRECT ZONE: Involves few or no coals and sits adjacent to the cooking zone. The indirect zone is ideal for low-temperature cooking and resting proteins.

When you build a fire with all three zones, you're fully in control. Here's how to do it right.

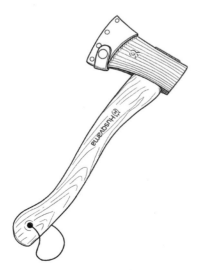

THE FIVE-STEP COOKING FIRE

1. Build or adjust your fire ring (be it rock, masonry, or metal) so it's large enough to accommodate all three zones as well as your grilling surface. Ideally, it's higher on the windward side. Once your ring's ready—but before you strike a match—make sure your grill surface fits and will sit level at the height you need.

2. Snug a larger log just inside the windward edge. Leave a gap of about 1 foot, then lay another larger log parallel to the first. The space in between is where your tinder will go. You can use wood shavings, dry leaves, pine needles, commercial fire starter, dryer lint—or a few sheets of rolled-up newspaper.

3. Now lay twigs, sticks, and other fast-combusting wood over the tinder.

4. Build up from the twigs to slightly larger pieces of wood, then lean even bigger ones tepee- or log cabin–style. (There's no wrong choice.) Light the tinder, do a little dance, add fresh wood as needed. For a thick bed of glowing coals, allow 30 to 40 minutes.

5. When you're ready to cook, set up your three zones. Push the burning logs to the area farthest from the windward wall (to make the burning zone), leaving coals and embers in the middle of the ring (for the cooking zone). The area nearest the windward wall should make a good indirect zone. Add your grill and you're good to go. For longer cooking jobs, you'll want to periodically rake fresh coals from the burning zone into the cooking zone to maintain the heat level; add fresh wood to the burning zone as necessary.

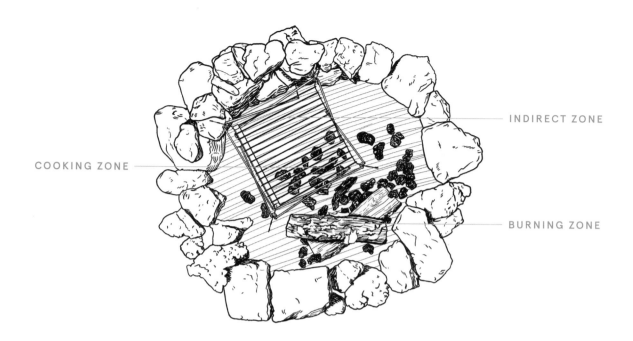

COOKING ZONE

INDIRECT ZONE

BURNING ZONE

HOW HOT IS IT?

The simplest way to measure the heat in your cooking zone is an admittedly not completely intelligent but nonetheless more-or-less-effective technique called the "hand test." Hold your hand around 5 inches (the height of a soda can) above your grilling surface, and start counting Mississippis.

FOR HIGH HEAT (around 500°F), you should be able to hold your hand there for 2 to 4 seconds.

FOR MEDIUM HEAT (around 400°F), you should be able to hold it for 5 to 7 seconds.

FOR LOW HEAT (around 300°F), you should get 8 to 10 seconds.

Just try not to, you know, catch yourself on fire.

FIRE GEAR

Live-fire cooking may be primitive, but your tools don't have to be.

FUEL

Large, crackling logs look and sound great, but they're typically slow to produce usable coals for cooking. Chop or break wood into thinner pieces—as wide as your forearm is ideal. These pieces are also easier to move when you need to adjust a fire's shape or heat, and you'll usually be able to cook sooner too.

FIRE GRATE

For trips where weight and bulk matter, I'm a big fan of height-adjustable roll-up grills. For car camping and cabins, a sturdy grate is also ideal. Stainless steel provides the perfect balance of light weight, durability, and corrosion resistance. Unless you've got a ton of cargo space (and even then . . .), leave the needlessly heavy, rust-prone cast-iron models at home.

HOW TO LEAVE NO TRACE

Even modest campfires can take a toll on fragile environments. Here's how to minimize their impact:

→ Use existing fire pits and rings wherever possible, or build your fire on a metal fire pan.

→ Never transport firewood gathered from outside the area. It can spread damaging pathogens and invasive insects.

→ Avoid cutting wood from standing or fallen trees, whether alive or dead. Instead, gather deadwood sticks and branches from the ground, or burn dry driftwood.

→ Burn your fires down to white ash, then douse them thoroughly with water.

For more information, visit the Leave No Trace website at Lnt.org.

TOOLS

A fireproof shovel, rake, or poker of some sort is a must for shifting burning wood and moving piles of coals and embers. Although purpose-built fire tools are nice to have, a stout stick will also do the job just fine.

Long-handled metal tongs are for everything your poker can't do. They're terrific for stacking embers and fine-tuning heat, placing coals under Dutch ovens and pans, removing lids, and saving dropped marshmallows from fiery doom. And yeah, you can also use them for handling foil packs and food.

Heat-resistant fire gloves should be in any live-fire cook's kit. Proper thermal-protection gloves are effective beyond 900°F and are widely available. Leather ranch gloves and standard-issue garden gloves, although nowhere nearly as protective, will do in a pinch.

If you'll be burning precut logs, you'll need a hatchet to split them. For thicker deadfall, you'll want a folding saw. For trips where I'm burning gathered sticks and smaller deadfall, I usually use just my foot to break up firewood—a well-placed stomp is typically enough.

How to Treat Water So It's Safe for Drinking

No ready-to-drink water where you're headed? No problem. These are the three most reliable treatment options if you're camping in North America.

FILTERING

Gravity filter systems are the best bet for families, groups, and higher-volume water users. They typically send dirty water, via a hose and filter, into a clean water bladder. Although they're larger and bulkier than some other options (typically around the size of a 1-liter water bottle and upward of 12 ounces), they're intuitive to use, highly effective, and work reasonably quickly (around 1½ liters per minute for the best of them).

Squeeze filters are as effective as gravity filters at cleaning water but are generally used for smaller volumes. Where they win out easily is their weight and size—around 3 ounces for better models, and small enough to easily fit in a pocket.

CHEMICAL TREATMENT

Chlorine dioxide drops and tablets rely on the same compound that's used in municipal water systems. They don't change the water's taste and are effective against a wide range of pathogens. A drawback: Chlorine dioxide takes four hours to kill *Cryptosporidium*, so whether it comes in drop or tablet form, it requires a bit of forethought. All the same, they're my go-to for high-mileage backpacking trips, and I always carry a few tablets as a backup in my paddle and car-camping kitchen kits.

GOOD OL' BOILING

A minute's rolling boil at sea level (or three-plus minutes at 5,000 feet and higher) kills common bacteria, protozoa, and viruses. But it can also take a ton of fuel and time, and once the boiling's done you've got to wait for your water to cool. For coffee, hot drinks, and water for cooking, it's my go-to option—you've got to heat it anyway. But as an everyday drinking-water treatment, it's a distant third choice.

How to Wash Dishes

Here's a simple wash routine that's as easy to use in the backcountry as at a drive-up site. As a bonus, it doesn't require bleach or a ton of soap, so it's gentle on the thing you came to be in—the wild. The sanitizing step is strictly optional. Many campers find it important. In the real world, it's not something I ever do.

GEAR

→ A lightweight, collapsible dish bin—or ideally, two if you plan to sanitize (Sea to Summit's 5- and 10-liter Kitchen Sinks are excellent)

→ A scraper-scrubber (MSR's Alpine Dish Brush is the gold standard)

→ Concentrated biodegradable camp soap (Dr. Bronner's Baby Unscented and Campsuds are excellent)

→ A few sheets of paper towels, fresh or used

→ A packable strainer

→ A reusable dishcloth (optional)

→ A cotton or linen kitchen towel (optional)

SET UP

Set up your dish station at least seventy paces (200 feet) from both your campsite and the nearest water source. Fill your dish bin with water (hot is good, but not mandatory). If you have a second bin and plan to sanitize, leave it empty.

PREWASH

Use a sheet or two of paper towel to wipe any loose food and grease from your dishes, then throw the towel in the trash.

SCRUB

Add a few drops of concentrated soap to your cloth or scrubber, adding more as needed. Always wash the cleanest dishes first, and save the dirtiest for last. If you plan to do a sanitize step, place the washed dishes in the empty bin, or let them drain on a rock or log.

DRAIN

To dispose of the dirty dishwater, pour it through your strainer to catch any bits of food (pack them out) and then broadcast the water over a wide area, at least 200 feet from your campsite and water sources. Rinse out the wash bin, if necessary, to get rid of any remaining grease or scraps.

SANITIZE (OPTIONAL)

Bring a pot of water to a rolling boil for one minute (longer if you're at altitude). If you haven't already, stack your dishes inside a clean bin. Pour the boiling water over the dishes and let them soak for two minutes. Remove from the water and let them air-dry. It's a good idea to then clean your scrubber and dishcloth (if using) in the remaining hot water.

Notes

→ Although some outdoors organizations still recommend a sanitize step using bleach, it's unnecessary in most circumstances, and it introduces corrosive organochlorines to your campmates and the environment. Biodegradable camp soap is a powerful degreaser—it lifts food residue, germs, and viruses off your dishes. If you're still really worried, give your dishes a one-minute sanitizing soak in 170°F (or hotter) water.

→ Biodegradable soap breaks down readily in soils, but it can last for years in waterways. Always keep it well away from water sources.

→ Once you're back at home, be sure to sanitize your dish gear: the bin, scrubber, and any cloths or kitchen towels. The Sea to Summit Kitchen Sinks can go straight into a washing machine.

Food Safety at Camp

Here's how to keep your campmates free from stomach upsets.

KEEP HOT *HOT*, AND COLD *COLD*

It's the first rule of food safety and the easiest to observe. Limit your camp food's exposure to "the danger zone" where bacteria thrive—temperatures between 40° and 140°F. That means anything meant to be cold—such as raw eggs, meats, sauces, and prepped raw vegetables—shouldn't sit out for more than two hours, or one hour in very hot weather.

And hot food should always be eaten hot.

When thawing foods, let them thaw in your cooler instead of out in the open.

And leftovers can get campers into trouble. Help them cool quickly by removing any wrappings (aluminum foil especially). Then, as soon as they've cooled, get them back on ice. Better still, plan your meals to avoid leftovers altogether.

AVOID CROSS-CONTAMINATION

Uncooked poultry, meats, fish, and eggs should be carefully wrapped so they don't cross-contaminate other foods in packs or coolers. Wash utensils, plates, cutting boards, and hands immediately after they've been in contact with raw, high-risk foods. It's always a good idea to keep a bin of dishwater and soap nearby. (See "How to Wash Dishes," page 41.)

POUR OUT SHARED SNACKS

Grubby camp hands and communal snack bags really don't mix. Pour chips, trail mixes, and other bagged foods into hands or individual containers, rather than have everyone rummaging through the same bag.

KEEP THE HAND SANITIZER FRONT AND CENTER

A huge proportion of "foodborne" camping illnesses don't come from food. They come from bathroom breaks. Wash hands thoroughly after visiting rest stops, and if that isn't possible have a container of sanitizer close at hand. I always set one out on the picnic table or in the center of camp, so nobody forgets.

How to Deal with Trash

There's no way around this: What you pack in, you have to pack out. But hauling a bag of rotting trash sucks when you're in the wild. With a few simple tips, you can make it far less of a pain.

PACK LESS IN, PACK LESS OUT

The easiest way to deal with garbage is to avoid it from the start. And no, you should not bury your trash, either—not ever. It's one of the best (worst) ways possible to train wildlife to seek out humans and their food.

PLAN YOUR MEALS AND PORTIONS WISELY

See "Making a Plan" on page 22, so you're never stuck with rotting leftovers.

DECREASE FOOD SCRAPS

Pack boneless meats and fish. And while fruits and vegetables with peels can't always be avoided (citrus and avocado are staple camp foods as far as I'm concerned, and cob corn is an undeniable treat), think through what you'll have to carry once the good parts are gone. Same thing with nuts—it's easy to pack shelled instead when you plan ahead.

If your stove runs on single-use propane canisters, consider using a refillable 5-pound tank and adapter hose instead.

Always aim to avoid single-use plates, straws, or cutlery and pointless plastics. And water bottles over bottled water every time.

STEP AWAY FROM THE FIRE PIT

Most outdoors organizations and land managers strongly advise against burning trash. Food scraps and packaging rarely incinerate completely, so they can quickly turn fire pits into critter magnets. That, and whatever's in your trash besides the obvious—the wax and plastic linings on many "paper" plates, for instance—can leave chemical residues that leach into water and soil.

FOR WHATEVER'S LEFT, CONTAIN THE STANK

I got by for years on heavy-duty trash bags, but I can't say those years were entirely incident-free. Leaking trash gets nasty fast. Instead, consider lining a rolltop stuff sack with a disposable bag or, better yet, try out Sea to Summit's purpose-built Trash Dry Sack.

How to Keep Your Food Safe from Critters Large and Small

The basics of bear- and critter-proofing your camp are pretty, well, basic. Keep food and drink far from your sleeping area. Keep your camp free from food scraps (no, those graham cracker crumbs under the picnic table are not okay!). And at night or any time you leave your camp, be sure to stash away anything with a scent—not just food but also soap, lotion, shampoo, toothpaste, deodorant, citronella products, booze, that shirt that got splattered with fish guts, and all your trash.

But how, exactly, to do that stashing is one of the most hotly contested topics in outdoor recreation. What works well in some parts of the continent with certain bear and scavenger populations can be useless just a couple hundred miles away. Here, you'll find a rundown of the most common solutions, along with their strengths and weaknesses. I've ordered them from the easiest and most accommodating options (i.e., the ones that make bringing good food into the wild easy) to the least. Which one you choose is going to depend on what kind of trip you're doing, where you're headed, and how much you'll have to stash. But if you don't know an area well, be sure to call ahead for best practices and requirements. Most park staff and land managers will be happy to help. In many areas, you can't get in without the right bear-resistant gear.

COOLERS

A growing number of hard-sided camping coolers are certified bear-resistant when fitted with simple bolts or padlocks. For car and RV campers (and paddlers with large enough boats and limited portaging): brilliant. For everyone else: sad face.

The Interagency Grizzly Bear Committee, a conservation-focused group that does the certifying, keeps a running list of approved coolers (and other products) at igbconline.org.

YOUR VEHICLE OR RV

If you're car or RV camping, you can generally stash food and other critter attractants in your trunk or hard-sided RV. Just make sure your car is locked! On one night alone in 2021, a black bear in Colorado broke into eight different unlocked cars.

BEAR-RESISTANT FOOD LOCKERS

Think high school lockers, but without the flirting or hairspray, and you have at least *some* idea of what bear-resistant lockers are. They're standard equipment in many US and Canadian wilderness areas, and because they put the gear onus on land managers instead of campers, they're also my favorite bear-proofing solution. They're even big enough, a lot of the time, to fit hard-sided coolers. Just be sure to check the dimensions in advance.

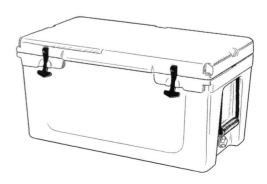

BEAR BAGS

Bear-resistant bags are fabricated from ultra-high-molecular-weight polyethylene, a material more commonly used to make body armor. The largest of them are nearly three times bigger than typical canisters, so you can pack in far more food and even some soft-sided coolers.

The downsides? Bear bags aren't yet approved for use in many popular areas. They're not all resistant to smaller rodents, either.

BEAR HANGS

A stout tree or pole, a length of line, and a bag to put your food in, and you've got a rudimentary bear hang. In many heavily traveled areas, the bears figured out bear hangs years ago; they're masters at shredding lines and snagging suspended bags in flying ninja leaps. (And that's even before the raccoons and opossums weigh in.) In other areas, including many alpine hot-spots, the trees aren't big enough to be of any use.

In spite of that, where I often camp around Ontario's Great Lakes, well-hung hangs are surprisingly effective. The pine trees are generally large and strong (hence more good branches for slinging lines over). And no offense or anything, but most of these bears lack the work ethic of their southern kin.

Some hang aficionados sling a line between two trees, then attach (or hoist) a bag mid-span. I typically throw a fifty-foot line with a pulley at one end over a high tree limb, at least five feet out, and tie it off. Then I run a second line, with my food bag attached, through the pulley and heave. Make sure that its lowest point (that includes dangling straps!) is at least fourteen feet up, and that it's no closer than five feet to the nearest tree.

BEAR BARRELS

Although popular with wilderness paddlers for their size, buoyancy, and ruggedness, these converted food barrels, which often come fitted with backpack harnesses, aren't going to stop your average bear. They're just not all that hard to open. I've seen raccoons get into them. Many trippers hang them for extra protection.

CANISTERS

These locking food containers are the gold standard in places with aggressive, educated black bear or grizzly populations, and they're required in many wilderness areas and parks. Fill them, close them, and then leave them out for the night—preferably far from your campsite. Bears can claw and chew them or pound them like bongos. Your food should make it through unscathed. For all those reasons, canisters are often the first (and only) choice for many backcountry campers.

On the downside, bear canisters are notoriously bulky in backpacks—yet somehow, they also can't hold all that much real food. (They seem to have been conceived with freeze-dried meals in mind.) Most of them can't even fit a small, soft-sided cooler bag.

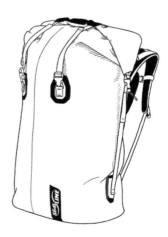

The One and Only Knot You Need to Know

This simple knot works great for 98 percent of camping jobs, such as rigging tarps, tent lines, hammocks, and bear bags, as well as tying up kayaks and lashing down gear. It's even ideal for attaching fishhooks to lines.

It takes a couple of minutes to learn, and seconds to tie. And with a single firm pull of the quick-release end, it undoes just like *that*.

Would I use it on a safety rope while traversing crevasses? For lowering booze or children down sheer granite cliffs? No and no. I definitely would not. (Although . . . what kind of booze is it? And who exactly *are* these kids?) If that kind of job is in your weekend plans, you'd best consult a non-cookbook for advice.

1. Loop the standing line—whatever your boat/tarp/tent is attached to—around your anchor point, then cross the free end over the top. Make sure to leave extra line at the end; about 12 inches for paracord, more for thicker ropes.

2. Pinch the intersection. With your other hand, wrap the free end around the standing line between three (for quick and dirty knots, thicker lines) and seven (for more secure knots, thinner lines) times.

3. Bring the free end back up toward the anchor point so the lines are parallel.
  For a quick-release knot: Tuck the free end's midpoint up through the opening to form a bend (shown in figure 3).
  For a non-quick-release knot (fishhooks, for example): Simply pull the free end up through the opening.

4. Now tuck the bend (or for a non-quick-release knot, the free end) down through the loop you just formed.

5. Tighten the knot. To untie, pull on the free end.

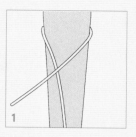

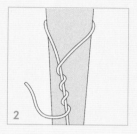

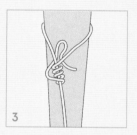

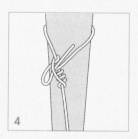

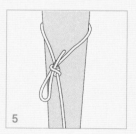

How to Use This Book

Most of the recipes in *Cook It Wild* are divided into two components: At Home and At Camp. In At Home, you'll find the ingredients and instructions for prepping ahead. At Camp details how to finish and serve each dish in the wild. (To help distinguish between the two, At Home ingredients and instructions are color-coded under orange headlines, while At Camp elements appear under green.) Each section has its own ingredients list, so be sure to read both before you leave for your trip. Any recipes that don't require pre-trip prep won't include an At-Home component. And recipes with no wild cooking required don't include At-Camp information. Just serve and enjoy.

In the Dinners chapter, you'll also find a few meals marked with a "Showstopper" ribbon. These are *Cook It Wild*'s most ambitious dinners, and, in most cases, they're made up of a standout main course as well as sides. Feel free, however, to mix and match; there's no reason you shouldn't make just one or two recipes from a showstopper menu if the full meal deal isn't feeling like your speed.

The symbols at the top of each recipe show what gear is required, as well as the types of trips they're ideal for.

GEAR SYMBOLS

→ No at-camp heating or cooking is required.

→ Requires a Dutch oven.

→ Some or all ingredients must be kept cold.

→ Can be cooked over a fire, usually (but not always) with a metal grill. Except for ash-roasted and Dutch-oven recipes, you can also use a gas or charcoal grill.

→ Can be cooked on a camp or backpacking stove.

TRIP SYMBOLS

→ Suitable for self-propelled campers. These recipes are reasonably lightweight and require no special equipment beyond a standard backpacking kitchen (see page 26), but they may benefit from a small, lunch-size cooler bag. Most backpacking recipes can be cooked on a lightweight stove. Some paddlers with limited cargo space or long portages will find these recipes most useful.

→ Suitable for most paddlers, as well as campers with some ability to carry bulk and weight. If a stove is required, a single-burner backpacking model is sufficient. Assumes access to a mid-size, soft-sided cooler.

→ Suitable for drive-up camping, RVing, off-grid cabins, or anywhere that transporting equipment and ingredients isn't seriously limited. Assumes access to at least one hard-sided cooler. Paddlers with lots of cargo space and limited portaging will be able to use many of these recipes.

IN-RECIPE SYMBOLS

→ You'll see this within many recipes' At Camp ingredient lists, to denote ingredients that can be optionally frozen at home, then thawed at camp.

→ Some recipes' At-Camp methods require skills or information from other parts of the book. The camera symbol marks those spots, so readers who won't be bringing the book camping can snap a photo before leaving home.

OTHER PLANNING FEATURES

Every recipe also includes its ingredient weight near the top. This figure includes all the ingredients in a dish but not packaging, optional ingredients, or water.

Keeps is denoted in each recipe and it indicates how long the ingredients in a dish can be expected to last. If the notation includes "kept cold," the ingredients should be stored in a fridge or cooler. Otherwise, ingredients can be held unrefrigerated, around 70°F. The time period of "Keeps" starts when the ingredients are prepped, so if you do that a few days before your departure, be sure to count that time. For anything that is frozen before departure, "Keeps" means how long it will hold once thawed.

The recipes state how many servings they make. The serving sizes are geared to average adult appetites and moderately active days. If you're planning energy-intensive travel and activities—or if you typically need more or fewer calories than the average person—adjust your packing accordingly.

A Few Ingredient Notes

The recipes in this book were tested to work best with Diamond Crystal Kosher Salt, except where noted. If you're using standard table salt, fine sea salt, or any other brand of kosher salt, use half the quantity called for, then adjust the seasoning.

All the butter in *Cook It Wild* is salted. It lasts longer at camp—salt is a preservative—and it tastes more buttery too. Unsalted will work just fine, however, if you prefer.

In recipes that call for extra-virgin olive oil, what you'll find at any supermarket is all you need. Some recipes where olive oil is a key ingredient call for "best quality" extra-virgin olive oil. You'll typically find this at specialty shops; if it's delicious to you straight out of the bottle, you've found yourself a best-quality olive oil. But if best-quality olive oil is beyond your means, standard extra-virgin is absolutely fine.

Raw garlic can pose a food safety hazard in prep-ahead cooking, especially when it's packed in oil and stored at room temperatures. Both are ideal environments for the growth of botulism, a dangerous bacterium. When a recipe asks you to bring whole garlic cloves to camp and add them there, please don't be tempted to prep it ahead.

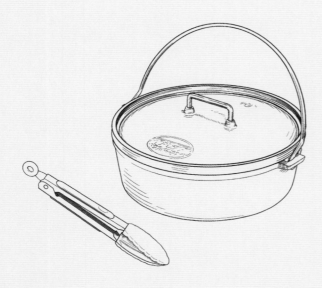

COCKTAIL SNACKS

(the Most Important Meal of the Day)

There may be no better moment than when you get to camp and drop your stuff—when the exertions of the journey give way to the feeling of we've arrived.

Late afternoon on a sun-warmed campsite is my idea of bliss. It's when you gather together after a day's adventures, or start to roll in if you've been on the move. You're hungry, though, I bet. Thirsty too.

It's the perfect time to open some snacks. Set out a platter of treats for the kids and a few plates of cheese and fruit. We'll pour out some candied nuts, or warm a little pot of fat, citrus-y olives that have been marinating for days. Open some chips and maybe a tin of good fish. Or some oozy cheese if it's early in the trip, set over high-summer tomato slices drizzled with Scotch bonnet–kissed honey.

And then there are always the premixed drinks: condensation-fogged cocktails and crisp, gluggable wine. We'll mix up juice crystals for the kids (don't forget the kids!) and watch them run feral. I don't know how afternoons can get better than that.

So, pull up a camp chair or a log. Shrug off that load. You're finally here.

Crunchy Rosemary Butter Nuts

Serves: 4 to 6
Ingredient Weight: 10 ounces

Buttery, brown-sugar sweet, and shot through with shards of rosemary, these easy make-ahead walnuts are some of the best cocktail (and trail, and after-dinner) nuts you'll ever try.

AT HOME

2 cups raw walnut halves

2 tablespoons salted butter (see Note)

4 teaspoons brown sugar

4 teaspoons granulated sugar

2 tablespoons water

1½ tablespoons fresh rosemary leaves, just barely chopped

¾ teaspoon kosher salt, or 1 teaspoon flaky sea salt

Freshly ground black pepper

KEEPS

1 week, unrefrigerated, or 1 month, kept cold

1. TOAST THE NUTS

Preheat the oven to 350°F. Place a baking sheet-size piece of parchment paper or a silicone baking mat on your counter.

Spread the nuts on a baking sheet in a single layer, transfer to the oven, and toast, stirring after 5 minutes, until they're golden, fragrant, and gently sizzling, 8 to 10 minutes. Watch them carefully so they don't burn.

2. MAKE A QUICK CARAMEL

In a large nonstick skillet over medium-low heat, combine the butter, both sugars, and water and stir with a heatproof spatula while the butter melts and the sugar completely dissolves, 2 to 3 minutes.

3. COAT THE NUTS AND ADD THE ROSEMARY

Add the toasted nuts to the caramel, stirring and tossing well to coat. Cook, stirring frequently, until the liquid has cooked off, most of the caramel has coated the nuts and the pan is mostly dry, 3 to 6 minutes. Turn off the heat, stir in the rosemary, and toss to combine.

Spread the mixture onto the prepared parchment paper or silicone mat so the nuts are not touching.

4. SEASON, COOL, AND PACK

While the nuts are still warm, season with salt and several grindings of pepper. Let cool completely.

Transfer the nuts to an airtight container and refrigerate or freeze. (They will keep for up to 2 months, frozen.)

Notes

→ For reasons that escape me, these nuts are far more delicious after they sit around for at least a day. So as tempted as you may be to snarf them all straight off the stove, avoid the urge.

→ To make this recipe vegan (and amp up the flavors!), replace the butter with 4 teaspoons of walnut oil.

Freakishly Delicious Olives, Warmed by the Fire

Serves: 4 to 6
Ingredient Weight: 19 ounces

Burbled gently with rosemary, chili flakes, and a squeeze of orange juice, these heat-and-serve olives become something else entirely. The warmth and gentle smoke transform them into the stone fruit they are—juicy, savory, deliriously fresh, superb with icy drinks.

AT HOME

1½ cups firm, green, pit-in olives, rinsed of brine

1 teaspoon chili flakes

1 sprig rosemary

½ cup extra-virgin olive oil

AT CAMP

Prepared olives

1 large garlic clove

1 small orange

KEEPS

1 week, kept cold

1. MIX AND PACK

In a leakproof container or resealable bag, combine the olives, chili flakes, rosemary, and olive oil and transfer to the refrigerator.

2. ADD THE FLAVORINGS

In a small pan, add the prepared olives and set over low heat. Smash and peel the garlic, then add to the pan.

Using a sharp knife or vegetable peeler, cut the rind off the orange and add the peel to the olives, along with 2 tablespoons of the orange's juice.

3. HEAT AND SERVE

Let the olives bubble gently for at least 5 minutes and up to 30 minutes. When they're warm and the smell is glorious, remove from the heat, squeeze in a bit more orange juice, and serve.

Note

→ The leftover oil is solid gold for frying fish or meats, or dressing vegetables.

Roasted Peppers
with Manchego

Serves: 4 to 6
Ingredient Weight: 27 ounces

Sweet, summery, smoky red peppers; prodigiously good olive oil; and milky-funky slices of Spanish Manchego cheese. Three-ingredient drinking food just doesn't come tastier than this.

AT HOME

3 large red bell peppers (see Note)

¼ cup best-quality extra-virgin olive oil

AT CAMP

Prepared peppers

Kosher or flaky salt

5 ounces aged Manchego cheese, sliced into triangles

A bit of crusty bread (a baguette or part of a sourdough loaf is ideal)

KEEPS

5 days, kept cold

1. EMBRACE YOUR INNER PYRO

If you've got a gas stove or grill, turn a couple of burners to high heat and place the whole peppers directly in or over the flames. Using tongs, turn them so they char evenly all around, 5 to 10 minutes. (Alternatively, you can prepare the peppers under your oven's broiler. Line a baking sheet with aluminum foil or parchment paper and place the whole peppers on it. Set the broiler to high, then place the baking sheet directly underneath the heating element, turning the peppers as needed for an even char.)

Transfer the charred peppers to a paper bag or bowl, close the bag or cover the bowl, and let steam for 10 to 15 minutes.

2. PEEL, SLICE, AND DRESS

Once the peppers have steamed, peel and discard their charred skins. (They should slide off easily into your hands, a paper towel, or the bag you steamed them in.)

Halve the peppers, strip out and discard any white ribs and seeds, and remove the stems and cores. Slice each half into three or four long strips.

Toss the pepper strips with the olive oil, let cool, and pack in a resealable bag or leakproof container. Transfer to the refrigerator.

3. SERVE

Let the peppers and their oil come to air temperature, then season with a fat pinch or two of salt. Place the peppers in a bowl or on a deep serving plate. Add the Manchego and toss so the cheese gets bathed in all the oily deliciousness. Serve with the bread.

Notes

→ With this few ingredients, use the best you can find and afford. Choose plump, dark-red peppers that feel heavy for their size; aged Manchego; and a fresh, flavorful olive oil, preferably unfiltered.

→ A tin of top-quality oil-packed anchovy fillets would not go astray here, if that's your thing.

Sizzling Garlic-Butter Bread Hunks

with Very Good Ham

Serves: 4 to 6
Ingredient Weight: 14 ounces

A really good crouton is hot and craggy and toasty-crunchy with butter and garlic, but still tender and softly sweet once your teeth break through. Drape it with a slice of excellent ham, then add some condiments to bring it all alive. Every bite's like getting away with something.

AT CAMP

½ baguette or small sourdough boule

1 garlic clove

2 teaspoons best-quality extra-virgin olive oil (thawed) ❄

2 tablespoons salted butter (thawed) ❄

5 ounces good-quality cured ham, thinly sliced (see Note)

A few assorted pickles and mustards (see Note)

KEEPS

The meat, up to 5 days, kept cold; the baguette, as long as it's chewable

1. TEAR THE BREAD

Tear the bread into crusty, soft-centered hunks, each around the size of a ping-pong ball.

2. SIZZLE IT UP

Smash and peel the garlic.

In a large skillet over medium heat, warm the olive oil. Add the garlic, butter, and bread pieces.

Fry the bread, turning the pieces frequently to coat with garlic butter, until it's golden and crunchy, 3 to 5 minutes.

3. SERVE

Discard the garlic, then transfer the croutons to some sort of vessel, along with the ham slices, pickles, and mustards. Serve immediately.

Notes

→ Any cured, thinly sliced pork product works great here: prosciutto, Black Forest ham, mortadella, jambon de Paris, Virginia country ham, or even jamón Ibérico.

→ The pickles and mustards cut the richness and saltiness of the butter and pork; you'll want at least one of each. A mix of sweet (bread-and-butter pickles), bracing (cocktail onions or green beans), spicy (British-style hot mustard), and crunchy-tangy (grainy mustard or Italian mostarda) is the pro move.

Creamy, Crunchy Chickpea Flapjacks, Cacio e Pepe—Style

Serves: 4 to 6
Ingredient Weight: 8 ounces

Farinata are super-humble flapjacks made from chickpea flour, a bit of rosemary, and a torrent of really good olive oil, fried up hot and crisp. But their texture and flavor are pure crunchy, creamy, woozy-making deliciousness. With a cold, crisp drink (slushy white wine's your best friend here) and a cacio e pepe—style blizzard of Pecorino Romano cheese and black pepper, this is the total fireside/lakeside/tentside fever dream.

AT HOME

1 cup chickpea flour (see Note)

1 teaspoon kosher salt

AT CAMP

Prepared chickpea flour mixture

1 cup lukewarm water

4 tablespoons extra-virgin olive oil (thawed) ❄

2 tablespoons chopped fresh rosemary leaves (yes, this seems like a lot; go with it!)

2 ounces Pecorino Romano cheese (see Note)

Freshly ground black pepper

KEEPS

The dry mix, up to 1 month, unrefrigerated; the cheese, 1 to 2 weeks, unrefrigerated

1. MIX

In a resealable bag, combine the chickpea flour and salt.

2. MAKE THE BATTER

In the resealable bag with the chickpea flour mixture, combine the water and 2 tablespoons of the olive oil.

Seal the bag, shake to mix well, and let stand for up to 8 hours.

3. FRY AND SERVE THE FARINATA

Set a 10-inch nonstick skillet over high heat. Working quickly, add 1 tablespoon olive oil and 1 tablespoon of the rosemary leaves to the pan and swirl to coat the bottom and sides.

Gently pour half of the prepared batter into the pan and cook until the flapjack is laced with air holes and nutty brown at its edges, about 2 minutes. (The batter will displace some of the oil when you pour it in.)

Slide a spatula under the farinata to dislodge any sticking bits, and shake the pan back and forth to release the farinata, then flip and cook until it turns crisp on the outside but is still slightly creamy in the center, about 1 minute more. Transfer to a warm plate. Adjust the heat if necessary (the skillet will continue to heat as you cook, so it may have gotten too hot), then repeat with the remaining olive oil, rosemary, and batter.

Cut the farinata into wedges, shave the cheese onto it using a vegetable peeler or knife, then dress with more pepper than seems reasonable.

Notes

→ The quality of different chickpea flours varies. I've had the best results with brands from Italy, easily found at Italian grocers or online.

→ These flapjacks make a terrific base for foil-roasted vegetables (see page 95), grilled chicken (see page 127) or steak (see page 150), or melty feta and tomato dip (see page 185).

→ Vegan option: Skip the cheese and top the farinata with fresh sliced tomatoes or any roasted vegetable.

Cheesy Tomato Hot-Honey Toasts

Serves: 4 to 6
Ingredient Weight: 29 ounces

I am a sucker for fire-grilled sourdough, smoky and golden and just slightly charry in places, brushed with a glimmer of olive oil. Set it out with high-season tomatoes, a bit of Scotch bonnet honey, and chopped burrata—the chopping makes the cheese even more voluptuously creamy. Everyone's drunk on goodness for the rest of the day.

AT HOME

1 teaspoon coriander seeds

1 teaspoon fennel seeds

¼ cup mild honey (such as clover or wildflower)

1 Scotch bonnet chili, halved and seeded (see Note)

AT CAMP

2 large ripe, flavorful tomatoes, sliced

½ pound burrata (excellent), roughly chopped, or Stracciatella (burrata's even sexier cousin) cheese

Prepared hot honey (thawed) ❄

Kosher salt

½ baguette or country sourdough loaf, thinly sliced

2 tablespoons best-quality olive oil (thawed) ❄

KEEPS

The cheese, up to 4 days, kept cold; the hot honey, 2 weeks, unrefrigerated

1. MIX THE HOT HONEY

Using a mortar and pestle, spice grinder, or a random heavy object, crush the coriander and fennel seeds into a coarse mixture.

In a small saucepan or microwavable bowl, combine the crushed seeds and honey.

Add the chili—half of it if you're spice-averse, or all if you like things very hot.

2. SIMMER, STEEP, AND PACK

Set the pan over medium-high heat or microwave the bowl on high power, bring the honey mixture to a boil, then remove from the heat. Let the mixture steep for 1 hour, then remove and discard the chili.

Transfer the mixture to a leakproof condiment bottle and refrigerate or freeze. (It will keep for 2 months, frozen.)

3. SET OUT THE FIXINGS

Prepare a platter with thick, sloppy slices of tomato, the cheese, hot honey, and a little dish of salt.

4. GRILL THE BREAD AND SERVE

Drizzle or brush both sides of the bread slices with the olive oil, then toast each side over a fire or in a pan, watching carefully so they don't burn.

Transfer the bread to the platter and serve immediately.

Note

→ The spice from Scotch bonnets lingers. For best results (and less capsicum-in-the-eyeball-induced hyperventilating), wear kitchen gloves while prepping the chili, and wash your board and knife well once you're done.

Campchuterie

Serves: 4 to 8
Ingredient Weight: About 3½ pounds

It's hard to argue with a heap of sliced meat, cheese, and fruit. For the cheese, use Pecorino Romano, Manchego, Beemster, or any other durable, delicious variety, plus an oozy soft variety if you plan to eat it within a couple days. As for the meat, cured sausages, such as capicola, Genoa salami, soppressata, and saucisson sec, are ideal. (Pictured on page 52.)

AT CAMP

A few nice cheeses

1 or 2 sticks cured sausage

1 pound fresh cherries or other stone fruit

A bit of fig jam, honey, or membrillo quince paste

1 sourdough baguette, torn or sliced

1. ARRANGE AND SERVE

On a platter, a sheet of wax or parchment paper, or beeswax food wrap, arrange the cheese, sausage, fruit, condiments, and bread, along with a folding knife. Dig in!

KEEPS

The unsliced sausage, 1 week, kept cold; the cheese, see "The Best Cheeses to Bring," page 16; the bread and fruit quit living their best lives after about 3 days

(Tinned) Fish and Chips

Serves: 2 to 4
Ingredient Weight: 18 ounces

Around Spain and Portugal, the best tinned fish is a bona fide delicacy; canning, at its highest level, is considered a form of art. Which all might sound like a lot if you grew up on tuna salad sandwiches. But conservas, as they're called along the Iberian Peninsula, can make for some seriously exquisite camp food. Pick up a mix of fish and shellfish, lay in a good bag of chips, and pair them with some Spanish hot sauce. It's high, it's low, it's conveniently portable. Welcome to pop-top paradise.

AT CAMP

2 or more tins of Spanish or Portuguese-style conservas

1 large bag top-quality salt-and-vinegar kettle chips (Lay's will do)

1 small bottle Salsa Espinaler hot sauce (optional)

1. SERVE

Pop the tops from the conservas. Set out some toothpicks for serving if you've got them. (Or if you're all classy, tiny fish forks.) Open the chips. Set out the hot sauce, if desired. The sauce goes on the fish, which goes on the chips. Salud.

KEEPS

2 months or more, unrefrigerated

"Welcome to the Party" Party Mix

Serves: 4 to 8
Ingredient Weight: 2 pounds

I was indifferent to party mix for most of my life. But then my friend Sasha, hoping to prove me wrong, built a version around chopped Medjool dates, with their dusky sweetness and satisfying chew. She added Spanish paprika and grated Parm for smoky depth, before I threw in extra butter (because *butter*) and a scoop of harissa paste for peppery, first-bite punch. And every handful of that reimagined party mix was suddenly can't-stop-eating-it delicious. I like to think I'm fashionably late.

AT HOME

6 tablespoons salted butter, melted

1½ tablespoons pure maple syrup or honey

2 teaspoons pimentón (Spanish smoked paprika)

2 to 3 teaspoons harissa paste (to taste)

2 cups roasted salted mixed nuts

1 cup salted corn nuts

1 cup pretzel sticks

4 cups Chex rice cereal

15 Medjool dates, pitted and coarsely chopped

One 1-ounce hunk Parmigiano-Reggiano cheese

¾ teaspoon kosher salt

Freshly ground black pepper

KEEPS

5 days, unrefrigerated

1. PREP AND COAT THE MIXTURE

Preheat the oven to 275°F.

In a small bowl, combine the melted butter, maple syrup, pimentón, and harissa and whisk to incorporate.

Place the mixed nuts, corn nuts, pretzel sticks, rice cereal, and dates on a baking sheet or roasting pan and toss or stir well to combine. Drizzle the butter-syrup mixture evenly over the party mix, stir well to coat, and spread the coated mix in an even layer across the pan.

2. BAKE AND DRESS

Bake the party mix, stirring every 5 minutes, until the mixture is toasty-golden and fragrant, 15 to 25 minutes. Finely grate the Parmigiano over the mix, then bake for 3 to 5 minutes more to melt the cheese.

Season with the salt and twenty good cranks of pepper.

3. PACK

Let the party mix cool thoroughly, then pack it in an airtight container or resealable bag. You can freeze the mix for up to 2 months.

DID ANYBODY FEED THE KIDS BOARD

The warm, gently salted young soybeans known as edamame are the stealth-healthy highlight of the fuss-free kids' board on the following pages. And the nori seaweed–based dry dip, called furikake, adds a beautifully sweet-savory crunch to fresh vegetables and stone fruit. Round it all out with a few kid-friendly faves (cheese strings and gummies never go astray), and your junior campers are going to be alright.

For the edamame, be sure to buy them frozen in their pods. They're precooked, so all you have to do is pack them frozen, let them thaw a bit (or not), and roast them in a hot, dry pan.

Dry-Roasted Edamame

Serves: 4 to 6 as part of a board
Ingredient Weight: 8 ounces

AT CAMP

½ pound frozen edamame in their pods
   (see Note; thawed) ❄

½ teaspoon kosher salt

1. DRY-ROAST THE EDAMAME AND SERVE

Set a dry skillet over medium-high heat. Once
the pan is hot, add the edamame and roast. Stir
or toss them occasionally, until they're warmed
through and the pods are nicely charred in spots,
5 to 7 minutes. Toss the edamame with the salt
and serve immediately.

Note

→ If your edamame are still frozen when you're
ready to cook, start them in a cold pan and warm
them slowly over low heat until they're thawed, 3 to
5 minutes. Increase the heat and roast as directed.

KEEPS

The unroasted edamame, 3 days, after thawing,
kept cold

Sweet-Savory Dry Dip

Serves: 4 to 6 as part of a board
Ingredient Weight: 3 ounces

AT HOME

½ cup white or black sesame seeds

2 small packs roasted, seasoned nori sheets

¾ teaspoon kosher salt

¾ teaspoon granulated sugar

1. CRUSH AND TOAST

In a mortar with a pestle or using a rolling pin,
crush the sesame seeds to release their oils.

In a medium skillet over low heat, toast the
crushed seeds, stirring occasionally, until they're
a light golden brown and roasty-fragrant, 6 to
9 minutes. Transfer the toasted seeds to a bowl
to cool.

2. MIX AND PACK

Stack the nori sheets, then using kitchen scissors
or a sharp knife, cut them in a crosshatch pattern
to make fine nori confetti.

Add the cut nori, salt, and sugar to the bowl with
the sesame seeds. Stir until well combined, then
pack the dry dip in a resealable bag or airtight
container.

KEEPS

1 month, unrefrigerated

AN ACTUALLY DELICIOUS VEGAN HUMMUS BOARD

If the only hummus you've ever known is the grainy, garlic-burpy, long-haul stuff from the deli section, this version will come as a shock. It's immaculately smooth and rich-tasting from a ton of good tahini, and the flavor is subtly balanced between chickpea-nutty and refreshingly tangy (so nice to beet you!). It's hard to quit eating it, especially when you throw in some flame-grilled bread. The trick is steeping the recipe's chopped garlic in lemon juice—a technique popularized by chef Michael Solomonov—then throwing out the garlic before it overpowers things. That and you boil the bejeezus out of canned chickpeas, which maybe seems like overkill, but mushy chickpeas equal magnificent hummus.

Pair the hummus with toasted pitas, a bowl of sizzling salted (shell-free!) pistachios, and an as-you-please mix of fruit and veg and your vegan board becomes a moment, the sort of spread your friends will ask for again and again.

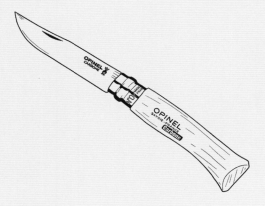

Silky Day-Glo Hummus

Serves: 4 to 6 as part
  of a board
Ingredient Weight: 29 ounces

AT HOME

1 medium red beet

1 teaspoon extra-virgin olive oil,
  plus more for topping

1 teaspoon water, plus ¼ cup

Kosher salt

1 cup drained canned chickpeas

½ teaspoon baking soda

2 garlic cloves, unpeeled

¼ cup lemon juice, plus more
  for seasoning

⅓ cup best-quality tahini

AT CAMP

Prepared hummus (thawed) ❄

Best-quality extra-virgin olive oil for
  drizzling (thawed) ❄

Lemon for squeezing (optional)

4 to 6 pitas, straight-up, warmed in
  a pan, or grilled

KEEPS

5 days, kept cold

1. ROAST AND PEEL THE BEET

Preheat the oven to 375°F.

Place the beet on a piece of aluminum foil, coat it with the olive oil, and add the 1 teaspoon water and ⅛ teaspoon salt.

Wrap the foil tightly around the beet, then roast until a fork pierces it easily, 60 to 90 minutes. Remove from the oven.

Once cool enough to handle, slip off and discard its skin, root, and stem with your hands or a paper towel. Coarsely chop and set aside.

2. SIMMER THE CHICKPEAS

Meanwhile, in a small saucepan, combine the chickpeas and baking soda, add enough cold water to cover by a few inches and set over medium-high heat. Bring to a boil, then decrease the heat to medium and cook until the chickpeas turn mushy, about 1 hour. Drain.

3. MAKE THE HUMMUS BASE

In a blender or food processor, combine the garlic (skin on!), lemon juice, and ¾ teaspoon kosher salt. Pulse to coarsely chop. Let stand 10 minutes.

Set a fine-mesh strainer over a small bowl. Add the processed garlic and press with a spatula to squeeze out the liquid. Discard the solids, then return the reserved garlic-lemon mixture to the blender.

4. WHIP AND PACK

Add the tahini, chopped beet, simmered chickpeas, and remaining ¼ cup water to the garlic-lemon mixture. Blend on high speed until the hummus is smooth. Add salt and lemon juice as needed.

Transfer the hummus to an airtight, leakproof container, top with a thin layer of olive oil, and refrigerate, or omit the oil and freeze. (It will keep for up to 1 month, frozen.)

5. SERVE

Stir the hummus well, then serve topped with a generous drizzle of olive oil, a squeeze of lemon juice, if desired, and pita bread.

Olive Oil Pistachios

Serves: 4 to 6 as part of
a board
Ingredient Weight: 2½ ounces

AT CAMP

1 teaspoon olive oil (thawed) ❄

½ cup shelled pistachios

Kosher salt

KEEPS

2 months or more, unrefrigerated

1. TOAST AND SERVE

In a medium skillet over medium heat, warm the olive oil. Add the pistachios and stir to coat in the oil. Toast, stirring occasionally, until they sizzle gently and begin to turn an appealing golden brown, 1 to 2 minutes.

Pour the nuts into a bowl, season well with salt, and serve immediately.

The 7 Habits of Highly Effective Wild Drinkers

Here's how to win at drinking in the wild.

1. Pack enough. But not too much.
Multiply the number of campers by the number of drinks they'll have per day by the number of days. Then add around 20 percent.

→ 12 ounces of beer is a drink
→ 5 ounces of wine is a drink
→ 1½ ounces of liquor is a drink

And remember: If you're camping in bear country, your drinks will need to stay out of harm's way at night and when you're not around. That flat of twenty-four tallboys may be a bit of a stretch.

2. Start as cold as you can.
Wine, cocktails, and noncarbonated mixers generally freeze well. Be sure to leave headspace in the bottles for the liquid to expand. Allow 48 hours of freezer time before your trip.

And if those bottles are insulated, leave their tops off in the freezer so the cold can get in. (For how to freeze beer, see page 84.)

3. Leave the glass at home.
Decant wine, cocktails, and spirits into light, reusable containers. Repurposed juice and soda bottles, Nalgene water bottles, collapsible drink bladders (HydraPak and Platypus both make great options), and vacuum-insulated bottles are all good alternatives. And if you're *really* into beer, a 64-ounce insulated growler is never too bad an idea.

4. Use blocks over cubes for your drinks.
Block ice stays frozen longer than cubed. Plus, when else does life let you wield an ice pick? But whatever you bring, keep your drink ice separate from your mungy, half-melted cooler ice; they're not the same thing.

5. Use the food cooler for food, and the drinks cooler for drinks.
Coolers that get opened for a drink every few minutes don't stay cool. It's far better to transfer a session's worth of beverages to a separate cooler—a collapsible, soft-sided one is often ideal—instead.

6. Dilution's the solution for iceless drinks.
Ever noticed how a cocktail gets better as it sits in front of you? As its ice melts, the water softens boozy edges. So, if you won't have ice, build that dilution into your beverage; add 20 to 40 percent cold water to your prebatched drinks. (This dilution is already built into the cocktail recipes that follow.) As a bonus, that water will help your cocktails freeze pre-trip.

7. Don't neglect the end-of-trip plan.
Anyone can drink well on Night 1 or 2. Keeping that up through Night 3 and beyond—when the ice is gone and you're left with only liquor—can be tough. But before you resort to that bottle of Everclear, think through what's actually delicious when it isn't cold. Whisky, rum, mezcal, and tequila are *meant* to be drunk at room temperature. Gin and vodka? Not so much.

Hot drinks (see pages 231 and 232) are also an excellent end-of-trip go-to. And a bit of citrus, whether fresh or dehydrated (see page 203), or powdered fruit juice (I'm partial to peach-flavored) can go a long way to making an end-of-trip drink tasty. Just don't tell your fancy mixologist friends when you get home.

Paper Canoes

Makes: 4 drinks
Ingredient Weight: 17½ ounces

The name, like the drink, is a shameless appropriation of what might be the world's most perfect cocktail—the sweet-sour-smooth, beguilingly bitter Paper Plane. Much (I'm only guessing here) like a canoe made from paper, these are ridiculous fun only while they last.

AT HOME

3½ ounces Amaro Nonino, Averna, or Montenegro

3½ ounces Aperol

3½ ounces bourbon

3½ ounces fresh lemon juice

3 ounces water (omit if you'll have ice at camp)

1. MIX

In a lightweight, resealable drink container, combine the Amaro, Aperol, bourbon, lemon juice, and water (if using). Freeze for several days before departure.

AT CAMP

Prepared Paper Canoes (partially thawed) ❄

2. SERVE

Serve straight up (or if you have ice, shaken).

Note

→ If you omit the water, you've officially got yourself a Paper Plane.

KEEPS

2 days, after thawing, kept cold, or 1 week, frozen

Ti' Punch

Serves: 1
Ingredient Weight: 1½ ounces

Ti' punch is a fixture around the French Caribbean, a few sips of tropical splendor (*ti'* is short for *petit*, French for "small"). The drink is made with local agricultural rum (rhum agricole), which is distilled from freshly pressed sugarcane juice, as opposed to the usual molasses. It's a brilliant backcountry camping drink; simple to make, strong but nuanced, delicious under the sun, and best consumed without ice. If possible, seek out dark rhum agricole from Martinique. Top brands, like Neisson, Rhum J.M, Maison La Mauny, and HSE, are increasingly available. Barring that, Haiti's Rhum Barbancourt is a delicious fallback.

AT CAMP

1½ ounces rhum agricole ❄

1 cube raw sugar or Demerara sugar

1 tiny lime slice (less lime is more)

1. MIX AND SERVE

In a small glass combine the rhum and sugar and, using the back of a spoon, crush the sugar and stir. Squeeze in lime juice, drop the rind into your drink, and sip away.

Note

→ You can stick the rhum in your freezer prior to departure to bring down your overall pack/cooler temperature, but it isn't strictly necessary for this drink. Ti' punch is typically served at room temp.

KEEPS

As long as your limes last

Fresh Lime Margaritas

Makes: 4 drinks
Ingredient Weight: 19 ounces

You _know_ you're going to want three.

AT HOME

7½ ounces tequila

5 ounces fresh lime juice (from about 8 limes)

2 to 2½ ounces agave syrup (to taste)

5 ounces water (omit if you'll have ice at camp)

1 pinch kosher salt (optional)

1. MIX

In a lightweight, resealable drink container, combine the tequila, lime juice, agave syrup, water (if using), and salt (if using). Freeze for several days before departure.

AT CAMP

Prepared margaritas (partially thawed) ❄

2. SERVE

Serve straight up, or if you have ice, on the rocks.

Note

→ Bonus drink! If you replace the tequila with bourbon and the lime juice with lemon, you'll get a very fine whiskey sour.

KEEPS

2 days, after thawing, kept cold, or 2 weeks, frozen

How to Chill Drinks without Ice

When the ice is long gone, here are two tried-and-true methods for chilling drinks. The first is as easy as a bit of forethought (and the right location). The second is basically a super-dorky science project—in which the science dorks get to drink cold booze.

DUNK AND CHILL

Stick your drinks and a few rocks in a sturdy mesh bag. Tie the top securely with a stout length of paracord (you do not want to lose it!) and a float of some sort, then lower the bag carefully into a cold river or lake.

COOL-VAPORATE

As water evaporates, it draws away heat. Evaporative cooling—the same phenomenon that makes a damp T-shirt feel chilly—can lower temperatures by more than 30°F. What does that mean for camp drinks? Wet a towel, bandanna, or your campmate's underpants; wrap it around a bottle; and then place it in a reasonably windy spot in the shade. Make sure the fabric stays wet, then wait a while. Although your drink is unlikely to turn to slush, this will lower the temperature noticeably.

Negronis for While You Set Up the Tents

Makes: 4 drinks
Ingredient Weight: 18½ ounces

A stone-cold classic around our camps, this version jacks up the gin quotient to keep the sweetness in check, while the splash of water softens the negroni's boozy edges, even without the usual ice.

AT HOME

7 ounces gin

4½ ounces sweet (red) vermouth

2 ounces Campari

5 ounces water (omit if you'll have ice at camp)

1. MIX

In a lightweight, resealable drink container, combine the gin, vermouth, Campari, and water (if using). Freeze for several days before departure.

AT CAMP

Prepared negronis (partially thawed) ❄

1 small orange, sliced (optional)

2. SERVE

If the drink is still frozen, a vigorous shake will usually turn it into slush. Serve straight up, or if you have ice, on the rocks. Garnish each with an orange slice.

KEEPS

1 week, after thawing, kept cold, or 1 month, frozen

First-Night Newspaper-Wrapped Beer Slushies

Serves: 2 (or 4 if you're really nice)
Ingredient Weight: 16½ ounces per can

If you're nervous about freezing beer, don't worry—I have a master of science degree (in journalism). And possibly more reassuringly, I do this all the time. (Just be sure to follow the instructions!)

You'll need newspaper for this method. Or paper towels. Don't use toilet paper—not a good look.

AT HOME

2 tallboys (16-ounce cans) gluggable beer, 5 percent alcohol or higher, at room temperature

1. FREEZE THE BEER

No more than 7 hours before your departure time, put the tallboys in the freezer.

2. PACK THE BEER

Remove the beer cans from the freezer and wrap each one individually in a few sheets of paper to insulate, and then, if you're the worrying kind, in a leakproof bag.

Note

→ Beyond 7 hours of freezer time, the risk of a beer-plosion increases dramatically. Same for low-alcohol beer and regular-size cans. So just don't.

KEEPS

The beer should stay slushy for up to 12 hours

DINNERS

We always end up eating past sunset.

That's never the plan—just the way it happens. The plan, every time, is to get ahead of dusk and the bugs, the dishes done by headlamp, the hurtle toward bedtime with teeth-brushing and kids needing stories, and the end-of-day symphony of zipping sleeping bags. Every trip, at least one of us says, Hey, let's be sure to get the bear bag hung before dark tonight. Anyway, forget it. The kids can stay up late. Stories? I'll make one up! The dishes will get done. Would you look at that twilight? Some things are more important than being on time.

Dinner at camp is one of the only times we're all dependably present. It's when we stop. When we're still. It's when the glow comes from fireflies and cheeks instead of high-resolution screens. Camp dinner in that fast-fading light is when we remember what being connected truly means.

Maybe because of that, those dinners in the wild have a way of becoming celebrations. This seems true almost no matter what the actual food is. It can be quick and humble—lentils and curry, or fire-warmed mac and cheese, or a plate of grilled vegetables. It can be a showstopping, ooh and aah–inspiring, multipart feast. No matter what it is, dinner is different. It's my favorite time of the day, and of the summer. Dinner at camp is when we make memories. In a lot of ways, they're the best ones of the year.

Sweet-Sour-Sumac Roasted Shallots

Serves: 4 as a side
Ingredient Weight: 15 ounces

Sublimely mellow and juicy-tender with a hint of smoky citrus from Middle Eastern sumac powder, these easy fire-roasted shallots go with pretty much everything and are as deliciously elegant as it gets. Heavy-duty, 18-inch-wide aluminum foil is best here; if you're using standard-thickness foil, divide the ingredients between two packets instead of one.

AT HOME

1 pound shallots (roughly equal size), topped, tailed, and peeled

¼ teaspoon kosher salt

½ teaspoon granulated sugar

1 teaspoon ground sumac

Freshly ground black pepper

2 tablespoons salted butter, cut into pieces (see Note)

6 sprigs thyme

AT CAMP

Prepared shallot packet

KEEPS

5 days, kept cold

1. FILL AND SEAL THE PACKET

Cut a double layer of heavy-duty aluminum foil that measures 20 inches long.

Arrange the shallots lengthwise down the middle of the foil, stopping 2 inches shy of either end. Add the salt, sugar, sumac, and a generous grinding of pepper. Toss to combine, then dot with the butter pieces and add the thyme.

Gather the long edges of the foil together, folding them over each other two or three times to form a tight seal. Seal both ends of the packet in the same way. Pack into a resealable bag or leakproof container and refrigerate.

2. ROAST AND SERVE

Place a grill over medium-hot coals with direct and indirect cooking zones.

Roast the shallots, shuttling the packet between direct and indirect heat as needed to maintain a gentle sizzling sound throughout the cooking. When the shallots feel very soft and a knife poked through the foil encounters almost no resistance, 25 to 40 minutes, cut open the top of the packet so you can see inside.

Finish the shallots over direct heat, monitoring them closely so they color in spots and the buttery shallot juices reduce to a glaze, 3 to 5 minutes. Serve hot.

Notes

→ The shallots can also be roasted without a grill by setting the packet in hot ashes directly next to medium-hot coals. Turn the packet frequently and monitor closely to prevent burning.

→ For a vegan version, substitute olive oil for the butter.

Miso Butter Radishes

Serves: 4 as a side
Ingredient Weight: 18 ounces

Roasting radishes softens their spicy edges, revealing pink and tender-sweet little orbs. They're beautiful with a glaze of miso and maple, refreshed as you serve them with lemon juice and salt. Heavy-duty, 18-inch-wide aluminum foil is best here; if you're using standard-thickness foil, divide the ingredients between two packets instead of one.

AT HOME

2 tablespoons salted butter,
   at room temperature

1 tablespoon pure maple syrup

1 tablespoon white miso paste

¼ teaspoon kosher salt

1 pound radishes, washed and
   tops removed

AT CAMP

Prepared radish packet

½ lemon

Kosher or flaky salt

KEEPS

3 days, kept cold

1. FILL AND SEAL THE PACKET

In a small bowl, combine the butter, maple syrup, miso paste, and salt and mix well with a fork.

Cut a double layer of heavy-duty aluminum foil that measures 20 inches long.

Arrange the radishes lengthwise down the middle of the foil, stopping 2 inches shy of either end. Dot the butter mixture evenly over the radishes.

Gather the long edges of the foil together, folding them over each other two or three times to form a tight seal. Seal both ends of the packet in the same way. Pack into a resealable bag or leakproof container and refrigerate.

2. ROAST AND SERVE

Place a grill over medium-hot coals with direct and indirect cooking zones.

Roast the radishes, shuttling the packet between direct and indirect heat as needed to maintain a very gentle sizzling sound throughout the cooking. When the radishes feel soft through the foil, 20 to 25 minutes, cut open the top of the packet so you can see inside.

Finish the radishes over direct heat, monitoring them closely until they're colored in spots and the miso butter reduces to a glaze, 3 to 5 minutes.

Transfer the radishes to a small bowl (or serve straight from the foil) and season with a squeeze of lemon juice and salt. Serve hot.

Note

→ The radishes can also be roasted without a grill by setting the packet in hot ashes directly next to medium-hot coals. Turn the packet frequently and monitor closely to prevent burning.

Beautifully Basic Mushroom Roast

Serves: 4 as a side
Ingredient Weight: 28 ounces

When you've got a nice pile of mushrooms and a campfire to cook them on, you're doing all right in life. These ones are roasty, juicy, and luxuriously concentrated—gorgeous on toast, stirred into heat-and-serve risotto (see page 110), or as a side. Use a mix of mushrooms for this dish— white, cremini, maitake, and oyster mushrooms are ideal.

Heavy-duty, 18-inch-wide aluminum foil is strongly recommended—at the end of roasting, you'll cut the packet open over your fire and sauté the mushrooms right in the foil.

AT HOME

1½ pounds mixed mushrooms, trimmed and sliced

2 medium shallots, peeled and thinly sliced

6 tablespoons salted butter, cut into pieces

12 sprigs thyme

½ teaspoon kosher salt

Freshly ground black pepper

AT CAMP

Prepared mushroom packet

KEEPS

3 days, kept cold

1. FILL AND SEAL THE PACKET

Cut a double layer of heavy-duty aluminum foil that measures 24 inches long.

Arrange the mushrooms and shallots so they run lengthwise down the middle of the foil, stopping 2 inches shy of either end. Distribute the butter, thyme, and salt evenly over the top. Season generously with pepper.

Gather the long edges of the foil together, folding them over each other two or three times to form a tight seal. Seal both ends of the packet in the same way. Pack into a resealable bag or leakproof container and refrigerate.

2. ROAST AND SERVE

Place a grill over medium-hot coals.

Roast the mushroom packet over direct heat. When they feel very tender through the foil, 20 to 35 minutes, cut open the top of the packet so you're able to stir the mushrooms with a pair of tongs.

Finish the mushrooms on the hottest part of your grill, stirring them as they sizzle, until their liquid has reduced to a buttery glaze and they're nicely browned, 5 to 10 minutes. Discard the thyme sprigs (or not). Serve hot.

How to Roast Any Veg in a Foil Packet

Foil-packet veg are a prep-ahead camper's best friend. They're simple to assemble, keep well in a cooler, and go straight onto the grill or the edge of the fire, zero dishes required. And as they cook, they turn sweet, melty, *and* woodsy-smoky. It's the kind of eating you can only get outside.

Every foil-packet veg roast should have at least three key elements: a vegetable (duh), a fat (butter or oil, usually), and a seasoning. But that doesn't mean you can't also add a creamy protein, like feta cheese (see Fire-Burst Tomato and Feta Dip, page 185). Or even meat (sliced beef with broccoli, butter, garlic, and soy, hello!) or seafood (shrimp with corn cut off the cob, butter, and Old Bay Seasoning, anybody?). A well-assembled packet holds about 1½ pounds of prepped ingredients. If you have significantly more than that, divide between two or more packets.

A double layer of heavy-duty, 18-inch-wide aluminum foil is your best bet. If all you've got is standard-thickness 12-inch-wide foil, keep your ingredients per packet to around ¾ pound or less.

TO ASSEMBLE THE PACKETS

Cut a long, double layer of the aluminum foil; most veg packets will need between 20 and 24 inches of foil. Lay the foil out in front of you. Arrange your ingredients so they run lengthwise down the middle, stopping 2 inches shy of either end. Gather the long edges of the foil together, folding them over each other two or three times to form a tight seal. Seal both ends of the packet in the same way. Label the packets with a Sharpie, pack them in a resealable bag or leakproof container, and refrigerate.

TO PREPARE YOUR FIRE OR BBQ

Set your grilling surface between 3 and 6 inches above the coal bed and arrange the coals so they end in a tidy line, for direct and indirect grilling areas.

Medium-hot coals are ideal. If you can hold your hand 5 inches above the grilling surface for 5 to 7 seconds, you're in the right neighborhood.

You can also roast foil-packet vegetables directly in the fire. Set the packets in the hot ashes next to the coals and turn them frequently.

TO ROAST

Vegetables that contain a lot of liquid (such as mushrooms, cabbage, radishes, tomatoes, and peppers) will generally roast best over direct heat. Dryer, denser vegetables (such as potatoes, squash, garlic cloves, onions, and shallots) usually do better over indirect heat. Gentle sizzling is always a good sign. Use tongs to turn the packets frequently for even cooking.

Soft, quicker-cooking veg, like asparagus, tomatoes, and radishes, will typically take between 10 and 25 minutes. For shallots, garlic cloves, shredded cabbage, whole small carrots, and other medium-firm vegetables, expect 30 minutes or more. New and fingerling potatoes and cubed squash will take between 30 and 40 minutes.

To test for doneness, slip a knife through the foil. The vegetables should offer almost no resistance.

To finish, cut a generous hole in the top of the packets so you can see in easily and steam can escape. Slide the packets onto direct heat. Grill between 3 and 10 minutes, monitoring them closely; you want the vegetables to caramelize nicely in spots and for any liquid to reduce and thicken to a glaze.

Roasted Red Cabbage Salad

with Oranges, Hazelnuts, and Feta

Serves: 4 as a side
Ingredient Weight: 40 ounces

This sweet, caramelized red cabbage salad gets glazed in luscious honey, butter, and burnt orange juices before being finished with fire-warmed hazelnuts and feta cheese. Heavy-duty, 18-inch-wide aluminum foil is best here; if you're using standard-thickness foil, divide the ingredients between two packets instead of one.

AT HOME

⅓ cup hazelnuts

1 pound cored red cabbage, thinly sliced

¾ teaspoon kosher salt

1 tablespoon balsamic vinegar

1 teaspoon honey

2 tablespoons golden raisins

6 orange rounds, ⅛ inch thick

6 tablespoons salted butter, cut into pieces

AT CAMP

Prepared cabbage packet

Prepared hazelnut packet (thawed) ❄

5 ounces crumbled feta cheese (thawed) ❄

Kosher or flaky salt

1 lemon

KEEPS

3 days, kept cold

1. TOAST AND CHOP THE NUTS

Preheat the oven to 350°F.

Spread the hazelnuts on a rimmed baking sheet and toast in the oven until they're deep brown and fragrant, 10 to 15 minutes. Rub away and discard any loose skins.

Let the hazelnuts cool, then coarsely chop or crush, seal in a small aluminum foil packet, and freeze.

2. PREP, DRESS, AND SEAL THE CABBAGE MIX

In a large bowl, combine the cabbage, salt, vinegar, honey, and raisins and toss well.

Cut a double layer of heavy-duty foil that measures 20 inches long.

Place the orange rounds so they run lengthwise down the middle of the foil, stopping 2 inches shy of either end. Distribute the cabbage mixture over the top, then dot it evenly with the butter pieces.

Gather the long edges of the foil together, folding them over each other two or three times to form a tight seal. Seal both ends of the packet in the same way. Pack into a resealable bag or leakproof container and refrigerate.

3. ROAST THE CABBAGE, WARM THE NUTS, AND SERVE

Place a grill over medium-hot coals with direct and indirect zones.

Roast the cabbage, shuttling the packet between direct and indirect heat and turning as needed to maintain a gentle sizzling sound. When the cabbage feels very soft through the foil, 25 to 40 minutes, cut open the top of the packet so you can see inside.

Finish over direct heat, using tongs to stir occasionally and monitoring the mixture closely, until the cabbage is glazed in buttery juices, has a few darker caramelized bits, and the oranges are deeply colored, 5 to 10 minutes. During the final few minutes of roasting, place the packet of hazelnuts on the grill to warm.

Transfer the cabbage mixture to a large bowl or platter. Top with the feta and hazelnuts, season with salt, and add a good squeeze of lemon juice (don't be shy—it makes this dish!) before serving.

Blistered
Herby Fingerlings

Serves: 4 to 6 as a side
Ingredient Weight: 27 ounces

Pretty much as good as potatoes get. This recipe makes two packets.

AT HOME

1½ pounds fingerling or new potatoes

2 tablespoons extra-virgin olive oil

½ teaspoon kosher salt

Freshly ground black pepper

4 sprigs rosemary

4 sprigs thyme

2 tablespoons salted butter,
  cut into 8 pieces

AT CAMP

Prepared potato packets

KEEPS

3 days, unrefrigerated, or 5 days, kept cold

1. PREP THE VEG

Scrub or rinse the potatoes and cut away any eyes or major blemishes. If using fingerlings, halve the potatoes lengthwise. If using new potatoes, halve larger ones as necessary so they're all roughly the same size.

2. DRESS AND SEAL

Cut two double layers of heavy-duty aluminum foil that measure 20 inches long.

Divide and arrange the potatoes so they run lengthwise down the middle of the two pieces of foil, stopping 2 inches shy of either end. Drizzle the olive oil evenly over the potatoes, season with the salt and pepper, top with the herb sprigs, and dot evenly with the butter pieces.

Gather the long edges of the foil together, folding them over each other two or three times to form a tight seal. Seal both ends of each packet in the same way. Pack into a resealable bag or leakproof container and refrigerate.

3. ROAST AND SERVE

Place a grill over medium-hot coals with direct and indirect cooking zones.

Roast the potatoes, shuttling the packets between direct and indirect heat as needed to maintain a very gentle sizzling sound throughout the cooking. When the potatoes feel soft through the foil and offer very little resistance to an inserted knife or skewer, 30 to 40 minutes, cut open the top of the packets so you can see inside.

Finish the potatoes over direct heat, reducing any remaining liquid (there shouldn't be much), until they color slightly in spots, 2 to 4 minutes. Remove the herb sprigs. Serve hot.

Burrata Poutine

with Durdy Gravy

Serves: 4 as a hearty side
Ingredient Weight: 2⅓ pounds

Fire-roasted, butter-bathed fingerling potatoes blanketed in burrata cheese and drenched in store-bought chicken(ish) gravy? It's high, it's low, it's appallingly durdy* and breathtakingly delicious. You're welcome.

AT CAMP

1 recipe prepared Blistered Herby Fingerling packets (see page 99)

½ pound burrata cheese

1 pouch just-add-water chicken gravy mix (see Note)

KEEPS

3 days, kept cold

1. ROAST THE POTATOES

Place a grill over medium-hot coals with direct and indirect cooking zones.

Roast the potatoes, shuttling the packets between direct and indirect heat as needed to maintain a very gentle sizzling sound throughout the cooking. When the potatoes feel soft through the foil and offer very little resistance to an inserted knife or skewer, 30 to 40 minutes, cut open the top of the packets so you can see inside.

2. PREP THE FIXINGS

Meanwhile, drain the burrata and allow it to come to air temperature.

Prepare the gravy according to the package instructions (this shouldn't take more than a few minutes). Keep warm.

3. FINISH AND SERVE

Finish the potatoes over direct heat, reducing any remaining liquid (there shouldn't be much), until they color slightly in spots, 2 to 4 minutes.

Arrange the potatoes in a serving dish. Remove the herb sprigs. Set the burrata ball over the potatoes and cut it into six to eight ridiculously creamy pieces.

Top with 1 cup of the warm gravy and get out of the way.

Note

→ I'm a fan of McCormick Chicken Gravy (it's branded Club House in Canada). It's nicely balanced and tastes a lot like homemade, without the acrid artificiality or crazy salt levels of most instant gravies.

---

* As opposed to "dirty." Dirty gravy is a Cajun specialty sauce that lovingly whisks a flour and butter roux with vegetables, aromatics, and a few pounds of ground andouille sausage. This is not that.

Simplest High-Summer Cherry Tomato Pasta

Serves: 4 to 6
Ingredient Weight: 42 ounces

Cook down tiny, peak-season tomatoes, garlic, and olive oil into juicy, bursting, noodle-napping goodness, then toss with a steaming mess of really good spaghetti. This is one of the easiest, most crowd-enthralling summertime mains going, with zero prep required. A mix of heirloom cherry tomatoes is the holy grail if you can find them.

AT CAMP

¼ cup extra-virgin olive oil, plus more for drizzling

3 garlic cloves, smashed and peeled

2 pounds cherry tomatoes

2 quarts water

1 tablespoon kosher salt

1 pound best-quality dried spaghetti (see Note)

A few fresh basil leaves, torn (optional)

Peperoncini piccanti or bomba sauce (optional)

Freshly ground black pepper (optional)

KEEPS

As long as your tomatoes last

1. START THE SAUCE

In your biggest skillet over high heat, warm the olive oil and garlic until they start to sizzle, about 1 minute. Carefully add the tomatoes. (It's all going to splatter a bit, so try not to lose an eye.)

Shake the skillet to coat the tomatoes with the olive oil, then decrease the heat to medium-high and cook, shaking the skillet occasionally, until the tomatoes are lightly browned on their undersides and some of them start to collapse, 4 to 8 minutes.

Using the back of a spoon or spatula, gently crush half the tomatoes, leaving the remaining ones whole. Decrease the heat to medium and let simmer, stirring gently as needed, until the crushed tomatoes and their juices have formed a sauce, 2 minutes more. Remove from the heat.

2. COOK THE NOODLES

In a medium saucepan over high heat, bring the water to a boil. Add the salt, then slip in the noodles. (If they don't fit all the way in, don't stress. With a minute's cooking, they'll relax like a spa-goer in a hot tub; you'll be able to gently push them in.) Using tongs, toss and stir the pasta, keeping the noodles separated.

Cook, stirring frequently, until the spaghetti nears doneness but is still assertively al dente, a minute or two less than the recommended time on the package. Remove from the heat.

3. PUT THEM TOGETHER

Place the skillet with the sauce over medium heat and warm to a gentle simmer.

Using tongs, transfer the cooked noodles from the saucepan to the sauce. If you're sloppy about it, they'll drip all sorts of starchy, salty water into the pan, which is perfect. If you're neat about it, well—neat doesn't always win, neat freak. You'll need to scoop about ⅓ cup pasta water into your sauce, or enough to loosen up the sauce.

4. TOSS AND SERVE

Using the tongs, toss the spaghetti and sauce all around until the starches thicken and the noodles are nicely coated, about 30 seconds.

Remove the skillet from the heat and dress the spaghetti with the basil, a drizzle of olive oil, a dash of peperoncini piccanti, and pepper, if desired. Serve immediately.

Notes

→ Look for a rough, sandpapery texture on the uncooked spaghetti, or the words *trafilata al bronzo* on the package. Both are indications the pasta dough was extruded through bronze dies. The upshot? That beautiful sauce will cling to the pasta instead of sliding off.

→ Browned tomatoes are good, so don't be shy about letting them caramelize. Browned garlic, on the other hand, tastes like garlic-flavored hairspray when it goes too far. If it gets too dark, just pluck it from the pan and discard, no harm done.

→ This recipe assumes you'll be using a single burner only. If you've got two, don't bother with the sauce and water burner-shuffle; you can heat the sauce and cook the noodles at the same time.

Small-Pot Pasta Is the Best Pasta

In camping life and in real life, pasta just doesn't need to cook in the massive pots of water you might have been told to use. Noodles cooked in a little water instead are far superior in important ways—provided you toss and stir them as they cook. That smaller volume of water gets super-starchy fast, which is perfect for finishing pan sauces. (The starch helps sauces cling to noodles.) And by consistently using the same volume of water and salt instead of randomly filling your biggest pot, you always know your noodles will be seasoned just right. Plus, for camping purposes, that smaller volume means smaller pots, requiring less time and fuel to heat them. My go-to ratio for 1 pound of pasta is 2 quarts of water with 1 tablespoon of kosher salt.

Pistachio Mint Noodles

(or What Some People Might Call "Pesto")

Serves: 4 to 6
Ingredient Weight: 21 ounces

Verdant with mint and basil, crunchy-toasty from pistachios, and melting with Parm and Romano cheese, this wild-cooking miracle-maker blankets any noodle (or veg, or meat . . .) like a warm, soul-stirring fog.

AT HOME

1 garlic clove, coarsely chopped

1 cup loosely packed basil leaves

½ cup loosely packed mint leaves

⅔ cup shelled, unsalted pistachios

2 tablespoons salted butter

½ cup best-quality extra-virgin olive oil, plus more as needed

⅓ cup coarsely grated Parmigiano-Reggiano cheese

⅓ cup coarsely grated Pecorino Romano cheese

Freshly ground black pepper

AT CAMP

2 quarts water

Kosher salt

1 pound penne, farfalle, linguine, trofie, or orecchiette pasta

1 portion prepared pesto (thawed) ❄

Freshly ground black pepper

Parmigiano-Reggiano or Pecorino Romano cheese for serving (optional)

KEEPS

3 days, after thawing, kept cold

1. MAKE THE SAUCE

In a food processor, combine the garlic, basil, mint, pistachios, butter, olive oil, and both cheeses. Season with pepper and pulse to form a coarse, slightly chunky paste.

Scoop the pesto into a leakproof container or resealable bag, top with a stream of olive oil, and freeze. (It will keep for 1 month, frozen.)

2. COOK THE NOODLES

In a medium saucepan over high heat, bring the water to a boil. Add 1 tablespoon salt, slip in the pasta, and, stirring frequently, cook to al dente, or until the pasta is tender but with a touch of bite left in its center.

Reserve ½ cup of the water from the pan. Drain the pasta and return it to the pan.

3. TOSS AND SERVE

Add the thawed pesto to the pasta and give it an energetic stir, slowly adding the reserved pasta water as needed to loosen the sauce into a creamy consistency. Season with salt and pepper.

Serve the pasta immediately, along with grated Parmigiano, if desired.

Rigatoni alla Super-Lazy Sunday Sauce

Serves: 4
Ingredient Weight: 3 pounds

Any good Italian will tell you the gorgeously meaty sauce recipe that follows is for *sugo di salsiccia*, but I can't help laugh-snorting a little whenever I hear that name. It's Italian sausage, a tin of tomatoes, and a few basic flavorings, basically as lazy as a Sunday sauce gets. At camp, it's strictly heat-and-eat: Cook your noodles, add the sauce. And everyone'll be calling you *nonna* by nightfall.

AT HOME

1 pound Italian sausage

One 28-ounce can whole tomatoes (preferably no salt added)

2 tablespoons extra-virgin olive oil

1 medium yellow onion, chopped

3 garlic cloves, chopped

¼ teaspoon kosher salt

1 tablespoon chopped fresh rosemary

1 to 2 pinches crushed chili flakes

Freshly ground black pepper

1. PREP THE MEAT AND TOMATOES

Using a knife, slit the sausage casings, then remove and discard the casings.

Put the tomatoes and their juice in a blender and pulse a few times on low speed to chop them up. Set aside.

2. COOK THE FLAVOR BASE

In a heavy medium saucepan set over medium heat, warm the olive oil. Add the onion, garlic, and salt, and cook, stirring frequently, until they turn soft and golden, about 5 minutes.

Add the rosemary, chili flakes, and sausage to the pan. Increase the heat to medium-high. Cook the sausage, stirring and chopping it with a wooden spoon to break up the meat, until cooked through and well-browned, 8 to 12 minutes.

3. ADD THE TOMATOES, SIMMER, AND PACK

Add the pulsed tomatoes to the pan with the sausage. Then rinse the blender with a splash of water and add that too. Using the spoon, scrape any stuck bits from the bottom of the saucepan.

Give the sausage-tomato mixture several good cranks of pepper, bring to a simmer, and then decrease the heat to low and cook at a burble until it's transformed into a lusciously meaty sauce, 20 to 30 minutes. Remove from the heat.

Let the sauce cool, then pack into a resealable bag or leakproof container and freeze. (It will keep for up to 6 months, frozen.)

4. WARM THE SAUCE, BOIL THE NOODLES

In a large sauté pan over medium-high heat, warm the sauce until it simmers. Then remove from the heat, cover, and keep warm.

In a medium saucepan over high heat, bring the water to a boil. Add the salt, then slip in the rigatoni and cook to al dente, stirring frequently.

AT CAMP

Prepared sauce (thawed) ❄

2 quarts water

1 tablespoon kosher salt

1 pound rigatoni pasta

Freshly grated Parmigiano-Reggiano
cheese for serving

Peperoncini piccanti or bomba sauce
for serving (optional)

KEEPS

3 days, after thawing, kept cold

5. PUT THEM TOGETHER AND SERVE

When the pasta is cooked, shuttle the sauce back onto the burner
for a quick reheat.

Reserve ½ cup of the cooking water from the pasta pan. Drain the
noodles and add them to the sauce, using a few splashes of the hot
cooking water to loosen the sauce if necessary.

Serve the pasta with freshly grated Parmigiano and a bit of
peperoncini piccanti, if desired.

Notes

→ This recipe assumes you'll be using a single burner only. If you've
got two, don't bother with the sauce and water burner-shuffle; you
can heat the sauce and cook the noodles at the same time (and rub
your head and pat your belly too).

→ For an even more super-lazy version, skip the onion, garlic, and
rosemary. It'll still be delicious.

Parm-Butter Noodles

with Charred Fresh Corn

Serves: 4
Ingredient Weight: 5¼ pounds

Fresh, fire-grilled corn and a tangle of good noodles swirled in a silky, buttery, ready-in-an-instant Parmigiano-Reggiano pan sauce. This straight-ahead but seductive summer dinner, inspired by Toronto handmade-pasta king Leandro Baldassarre, is one of the most life-affirming noodle dishes I know.

AT CAMP

4 cobs fresh corn, in the husks

2 quarts water

1 tablespoon kosher salt

1 pound dry, straight fettuccine pasta (see Note)

8 tablespoons salted butter, cut into pieces (thawed) ❄

1⅓ cups finely grated Parmigiano-Reggiano cheese

KEEPS

The corn lasts several days unrefrigerated, but will be at its best for no more than 3 days, kept cold

1. ROAST THE CORN

On a medium-hot grill or at the edge of a fire, roast the corn in its husks, rotating the cobs frequently, until the kernels are tender and charred in spots, 10 to 15 minutes. (Alternately, husk the corn and boil to tender-crisp, 4 to 5 minutes.) Remove from the heat.

Husk the corn, cut the kernels off the cobs, and set aside.

2. COOK THE NOODLES

In a medium saucepan over high heat, bring the water to a boil. Add the salt and fan the pasta into the pan. Cook to al dente, stirring and tossing frequently. Remove the pan from the burner (but don't drain).

3. PUT IT ALL TOGETHER AND SERVE

In a large skillet over medium heat, combine the butter and ½ cup of the pasta water, then use tongs to add the cooked noodles. Simmer gently, tossing and stirring the noodles to coat while the butter melts, the sauce forms a uniform emulsion, and the starches in the pan thicken, 1 to 2 minutes.

Remove from the heat and continue tossing while sprinkling the cheese into the mix. Slowly stir in up to 1 cup of the reserved pasta water, as needed, to incorporate the cheese and loosen the mixture to a saucy (but not soupy) consistency.

Divide the pasta among four bowls and top with the roasted corn. Serve immediately.

Notes

→ As with the tomato pasta on page 102, look for bronze die-extruded noodles. A sauce this simple wants something nice to hold on to (don't we all?). It'll make a considerable difference in the final dish.

→ Cheese sauces this basic do not respond well to delays. Make sure your people are ready to eat before you serve.

→ Some recipes (like this one!) are so easy that prepping ahead feels unnecessary. That said, the corn here can be roasted or boiled at home, then packed. It'll be fine for up to 3 days if kept cold. The cheese can be grated ahead of time and frozen too.

Instant Fancy-Restaurant Risotto

Serves: 4 as a hearty side
Ingredient Weight: 22 ounces

You know the place. The super-fancy, old-guard Italian spot that every big city seems to have, the one where the fish is always caught that very morning, the truffles are always from Alba (even out of season), and the risotto—or so the servers never fail to mention—is always made to order, especially for *you*. I can't speak for certain as to the fish and truffles, but restaurant risotto is *never* made to order—not even at its most luxuriously buttery-cheesy-dreamy best. It's precooked, then reheated for your order. Also, truly great risotto is roughly twenty times easier than you've possibly been led to believe (see page 113). Which all makes it some seriously outstanding dump-and-stir camping food.

AT HOME

4 cups low-sodium chicken stock or vegetable stock

3 tablespoons salted butter

1 medium shallot, peeled and finely chopped

1 cup carnaroli rice

⅓ cup dry white wine

1 cup finely grated Parmigiano-Reggiano cheese

Freshly ground black pepper

1. PREP YOUR GEAR AND INGREDIENTS

In a small saucepan over medium-high heat, warm the chicken stock to a simmer, then decrease the heat to low.

Meanwhile, line a baking sheet with parchment paper and set it near the stove.

2. BUILD YOUR BASE

In a heavy medium saucepan over medium-low heat, melt 1 tablespoon of the butter, then add the shallot. Cook, stirring frequently, until it is soft and fragrant but not browned, about 2 minutes.

Add the rice to the pan and toast, stirring constantly, until the grains are translucent at their tips, 2 to 3 minutes. Increase the heat to medium, pour in the wine, and stir until the liquid is almost entirely absorbed by the rice.

3. LADLE, STIR, AND REPEAT

One ladleful at a time, start adding the hot stock to the rice, stirring continually. Wait for the rice to absorb each new addition of stock before adding another. Once your pot of stock is two-thirds empty—around the 15-minute mark—start tasting the risotto for doneness. Continue adding stock and stirring until the rice grains are creamy on their outsides and just slightly chalky in their middles. (You won't necessarily use all your stock and that's okay.)

4. QUICK-COOL AND PACK

Transfer the rice to the prepared baking sheet, spreading it into a thin layer. Refrigerate the risotto until cool.

Fold up the parchment to envelop the risotto in a little package. Seal in a resealable bag or container and refrigerate.

AT CAMP

Prepared risotto

2 cups water

Prepared Cheesy Butter, cut into
    pieces (thawed) ❄

Kosher salt

1 recipe roasted mushrooms or shallots
    (see page 88 or 92; optional)

KEEPS

5 days, kept cold

5. PREP THE CHEESY BUTTER

In a medium bowl, combine the cheese, remaining 2 tablespoons butter, and a few grindings of pepper and, using a fork, stir and mash the mixture until it's well incorporated. Transfer the mixture onto a sheet of parchment paper or thin plastic wrap, roll tightly into a log, and freeze.

6. REHEAT, SEASON, AND SERVE

In a medium saucepan over medium heat, combine the risotto and 1 cup of the water, stirring frequently until the rice is loose (but not soupy) and heated through, 3 to 5 minutes.

Taste for doneness. In ¼ cup-increments, add up to the remaining 1 cup water, stirring constantly, to cook the rice grains so they're slightly firm in the center but not chalky.

Add the cheesy butter to the risotto and stir well to melt and combine. Season with salt, then top with the roasted vegetables, if desired. Serve immediately.

Note
→ For a bright and sunny lemon-pepper version, make the Cheesy Butter as directed, but add the zest of 1 lemon and 2 teaspoons lemon juice, plus many good cranks of black pepper.

Five Tips to Perfect Make-Ahead Risotto

With these five simple steps, you'll be a master of risotto in the wild.

1. Leave the Arborio, take the carnaroli.
Arborio rice, which most risotto recipes call for, goes mushy in a flash; carnaroli rice is far more forgiving, especially for reheating. You can find it at Italian specialty grocers or online.

2. Risotto waits for no one.
Have everything ready and at hand before you start the prep cooking.

3. Can't stop, don't stop stirring.
Every loop your spatula makes around and through the pot not only keeps the rice from sticking, but also makes your risotto more lusciously creamy. It's 20 minutes of your life. Spend it well.

4. Undercooked risotto at home equals perfect risotto at camp.
So, go for rice grains that are creamy on the outside and just slightly chalky on the inside when you prep the dish.

5. Season only at the end.
The salt in your stock concentrates as the risotto cooks. The Parmigiano-Reggiano cheese you'll add boosts the saltiness even more. Wait to season (if your risotto even needs it) until immediately before serving. You'll nail it every time.

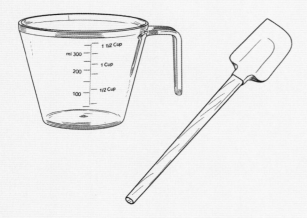

Wildly Delicious
Mac and Cheese

Serves: 4
Ingredient Weight: 2¾ pounds

Make it at home and pack into aluminum takeout containers. Stick them straight on the grill, then bask in your campmates' joy.

SPECIAL EQUIPMENT

Two aluminum takeout pans;
6½ by 4½ inches is ideal

AT HOME

2 quarts water

3½ teaspoons kosher salt

8 ounces macaroni

¼ cup salted butter

¼ cup all-purpose flour

2 cups milk

1 cup coarsely grated Gruyère cheese

2 cups coarsely grated
    cheddar cheese

Scant ⅛ teaspoon cayenne pepper

Scant ⅛ teaspoon grated fresh
    nutmeg

AT CAMP

Prepared mac-and-cheese pans
    (thawed) ❄

KEEPS

3 days, after thawing, kept cold

1. BOIL THE PASTA

In a medium saucepan over high heat, bring the water to a boil. Add 1 tablespoon of the salt and the macaroni and cook for three-fourths of the lowest recommended time on the package. (If it says 8 to 10 minutes, for example, cook it for 6 minutes.)

Drain the macaroni, rinse well with cold water, and set aside.

2. MAKE THE SAUCE

In a medium saucepan over medium-low heat, melt the butter, 1 to 2 minutes. Add the flour, whisking until the mixture smells faintly nutty and has turned from light blond to light golden brown, 2 to 4 minutes.

Remove the pan from the heat, slowly whisk in the milk, then return the pan to the burner. Increase the heat to medium and bring to a simmer, whisking, until the sauce is smooth and thickened, 2 to 3 minutes.

Remove the pan from the heat and stir in both cheeses, the cayenne, nutmeg, and remaining ½ teaspoon salt. Let the sauce cool for 15 minutes.

3. PUT IT ALL TOGETHER

Cut two sheets of aluminum foil to cover the aluminum pans, then butter one side of each sheet. Butter the bottom and sides of the aluminum pans.

Transfer the cooked macaroni into the sauce and stir to combine. (The mixture will look sauce-heavy until it's reheated.)

Divide the mixture between the prepared pans. Cover tightly with the foil. Pack the pans in a resealable bag and refrigerate or freeze. (The mac and cheese will keep for 1 month, frozen.)

4. GRILL AND SERVE

Place the covered pans on a grill over medium heat, rotating them occasionally until the mac and cheese is hot and bubbly throughout, 15 to 20 minutes. Serve immediately.

Long-Haul
Red Lentil Dal

Serves: 4, with a starch
Ingredient Weight: 14 ounces

I made this warming, protein-packed, and intensely comforting dish (pictured on page 2) in Jasper National Park's iconic Tonquin Valley a few Septembers ago. It was late in the hiking season; we'd woken that morning with ice in the tent. The peaks of the Ramparts, the mountain chain to the valley's west, were newly heavy with snow. Yet even there, in a remote, hike-in campsite with far more caribou than campers, a pot of lentils this good draws a crowd. Before we'd even started eating, my hiking pal Toby was dishing out little sampler bowls of the stuff for a half dozen hungry hangers-on.

What struck me then—and still strikes me today—is how amazed they all were that you could eat this well in a place like that. How every one of them, half-crazed from subsisting on insipid just-add-water entrées, asked some version of "Where did you buy this stuff?"

That dal, adapted from a recipe by Indian food expert and blogger Hari Ghotra, is one of the easiest go-anywhere dishes that I know. You cook the curry paste—the masala—at home, then simply stir it into quick-cooking lentils. It takes a single pot and 10 minutes and weighs less than 4 ounces per serving, or just slightly more with a few sachets of instant rice.

1. TOAST THE SPICES; COOK THE ONIONS

In a medium saucepan over medium heat, warm the vegetable oil and butter. Add the cumin, bay leaf, and dried chilis and cook for 1 minute, swirling the pan occasionally to keep everything moving.

Add the onion, garlic, and 1½ teaspoons salt to the pan and cook, stirring occasionally, until the onion turns an appealing golden brown, 6 to 8 minutes.

2. ADD THE VEG AND COOK IT ALL DOWN

Place a box grater over a medium bowl. Using the coarse side, grate the tomatoes; the pulp will fall into the bowl while the skin and stems (which you'll discard) stay in your hand.

Add the tomato pulp, grated ginger, and chopped jalapeño to the pan along with the turmeric, garam masala, and fenugreek. Cook, stirring occasionally, until the tomatoes' liquid has mostly evaporated, 3 to 5 minutes. Add the water and stir well, using a wooden spoon to coax any sticky bits from the bottom of the pan.

Decrease the heat to low and cook the masala at a very mellow sizzle, stirring occasionally, until most of its moisture has cooked off and it smells richly warm and fragrant, 20 to 25 minutes. Remove from the heat.

Let the paste cool, then pack it in a resealable bag or container and freeze. (It will keep for 1 month, frozen.)

1 tablespoon vegetable oil

1 tablespoon salted butter (see Note)

1 teaspoon cumin seeds

1 bay leaf

2 dried red chilies, or ½ teaspoon chili flakes

1 medium yellow onion, chopped

1 garlic clove, finely chopped

Kosher salt

2 medium tomatoes

1 teaspoon finely grated ginger

½ jalapeño chili, stemmed, seeded, and finely chopped

1 teaspoon turmeric powder

1 teaspoon garam masala

1 teaspoon dried fenugreek seeds

½ cup water

AT CAMP

1 quart water

1 cup split red lentils, picked through for stones and debris

Prepared curry paste (thawed) ❄

1 small bunch cilantro

1 lime

Cooked rice, potatoes, or chapati (see page 142) for serving (optional)

KEEPS

The masala, 3 days, unrefrigerated, or up to 7 days, kept cold

3. COOK THE LENTILS

In a small pot over high heat, combine the water and lentils and bring to a boil, scooping off any thick foam.

Decrease the heat to medium and cook the lentils until very tender but still mostly intact, 7 to 10 minutes.

Reserve ¾ cup of the hot cooking water from the pot.

4. DRAIN, DRESS, AND SERVE

Drain half of the lentils' remaining water, then return the pot to the burner and add the curry paste, stirring to mix and heat it through. If you like a soupier bowl of lentils, add back some or all of the reserved cooking water, adjusting the seasoning accordingly (it will likely need a few pinches of salt). If you prefer them thicker, add only a few teaspoons of water as needed.

Serve the dal with a handful of chopped or torn cilantro leaves and a squeeze of lime juice on top, paired with rice, potatoes, or chapati, if desired.

Note
→ For a vegan option, use 1 tablespoon melted coconut oil in place of the butter.

Saucy, Cidery, Shallot-y Baked Beans

Serves: 8
Ingredient Weight: 5 pounds

What do you get when you make baked beans saucy and tender instead of dry and pasty? When you balance them perfectly between sweet, meaty, and sour so they're darkly rich like the baked beans you've always known, but also beguilingly fresh? These make-ahead, slow-baked sweet beans update the campfire classic for an age that takes its beans seriously. They're loaded with juicy pork hock, melting balsamic-marinated shallots, and a seam of apple cider vinegar and orange zest to keep their richness in check. And although their start-to-finish time spans a couple of days—the dry beans and shallots get an overnight soak—that's almost entirely hands-off time.

In any case, sure, I have a few relatives who might grumble that it's easier to open a tin and put it on the fire. Maybe you do too. But these are not your crusty uncle's franks and beans. Just hand anyone a bowl and watch their eyes bug out with begrudging joy. And probably don't mention the orange zest part.

AT HOME

1 pound dried navy beans

¾ pound medium shallots, topped, tailed, and peeled

1 cup water, plus more for soaking beans

3 tablespoons apple cider vinegar

3 tablespoons balsamic vinegar

1. THE NIGHT BEFORE, SOAK THE BEANS

Give the dry beans a once-over, discarding any stones and beans that are broken, shriveled, or badly discolored.

In a large bowl, combine the beans with cold water to cover by 2 inches and let soak overnight.

2. AND ALSO THE SHALLOTS

Meanwhile, cut the shallots in half lengthwise, then cut each half in two at its waist.

In a small container, tightly pack the cut shallots, then add the water, apple cider vinegar, balsamic vinegar, sugar, ¼ teaspoon of the salt, and orange zest. (The liquid should cover most or all of the shallots.) Stir the mixture well, cover, and refrigerate overnight.

3. PREP AND COOK THE FLAVOR BASE

Preheat the oven to 350°F.

Cut three of the bacon slices into ¼-inch pieces. In a 7-quart (or larger) ovenproof pot, combine the bacon pieces and vegetable oil. Set over medium heat and render some of the fat, about 2 minutes. Add the onion, garlic, and ¼ teaspoon salt and cook, stirring frequently, until the vegetables turn tender and begin to brown, 5 to 8 minutes.

Decrease the heat to low, add the tomato paste to the pot, and cook, stirring frequently with a sturdy wooden spoon, until it turns a deep bricky-red and smells like bacon-tomato caramel, 5 to 8 minutes. (Some of the paste will stick to the bottom of the pot. That's okay.)

Pour the marinated shallots and their liquid into the pot and increase the heat to medium-high. Using a wooden spoon, scrape any stuck bits from the bottom of the pot and stir into the mix.

4. BUILD THE BEANS

Drain the soaked beans and add them to the pot, along with 10 cups water, and increase the heat to high. Add the mustard powder, thyme sprigs, bay leaves, and ten good cranks of pepper. Stir well to combine.

¼ cup packed Demerara sugar or
    dark brown sugar

1½ teaspoons kosher salt

Zest of ½ orange

6 slices bacon

1 tablespoon vegetable oil

1 medium yellow onion, chopped

3 garlic cloves, minced

½ cup canned tomato paste, or
    ¼ cup double-concentrated tubed
    tomato paste

1 teaspoon hot mustard powder

6 sprigs thyme

2 bay leaves, fresh (best) or
    dried (fine)

Freshly ground black pepper

One 1-pound piece smoked ham hock
    or other smoked pork product
    (see Note)

AT CAMP

Prepared beans (thawed) ❄

1 tablespoon water per serving

A few frankfurter wieners (optional)

KEEPS

3 days, kept cold

Snug the ham hock into the beans (if it sticks way out of the liquid, feel free to cut it into several pieces). Cut the remaining three bacon slices into 2-inch pieces and scatter them over the beans.

5. BAKE AND SEASON

Once the beans come to a simmer, place the pot in the oven, uncovered. After 2 hours, add the remaining 1 teaspoon salt, sprinkling it over the top to distribute evenly. Bake for 2½ to 3½ hours more, or until the beans are beautifully tender, the shallots are melty, and the meat is falling apart, but a few cups of broth remain. (The liquid will be absorbed as the beans cool, so avoid the temptation to bake until dry.)

Remove and discard the thyme and bay leaves. Transfer the ham hock to a cutting board, and discard the bone, fat, and any skin. Pull apart the meat into bite-size bits, then add back to the pot and give it a gentle stir.

6. PACK

Pack the beans into a reusable container, resealable bag, or, if you plan to reheat them on a grill, an aluminum takeout tray and then cover with aluminum foil. (If your party's smaller than eight people, pack 8 to 10 ounces of beans per serving.) Refrigerate or freeze. (They will keep for 1 month, frozen.)

7. REHEAT AND SERVE

On a grill (if packed in foil) or in a saucepan over medium-low heat, gently warm the beans, adding the water, as needed, to bring to a saucy consistency.

If adding wieners, grill them or simply tuck into the beans while reheating to warm. Serve immediately.

Note

→ If you can't find a 1-pound ham hock, have your butcher cut down a larger one for you. Although ham hock is ideal here, feel free to substitute 1 pound of any smoked pork product, provided it hasn't been sauced or heavily dry-rubbed. A hunk of double-smoked belly, jowl, or ribs will be no slouch.

Cooking While High

(on That Sweet, Sweet Altitude)

Above and beyond 2,500 feet, the lower air pressure starts to change how long it takes for food to cook, how quickly liquids evaporate, how baked goods rise, and how hard your stove has to work. Here's how to navigate those heights.

PLAN FOR LONGER COOKING TIMES

For every 500 feet of elevation, water's boiling point drops by around 1°F. Whatever food you put in it will take longer to cook. (And nope, cranking up your stove's output will not change a thing—except how quickly you burn through gas.)

Up to 2,500 feet, you'll barely notice a change. At 10,000 feet, it takes 25 percent longer to soft-cook an egg. Keep this in mind for your fuel calculations.

EXPECT MORE EVAPORATION

Water evaporates faster at elevation. So, plan to go through more of it when boiling food. And that quick evaporation, combined with drier air, can swiftly dry out proteins and baked goods too.

COOK PROTEINS WITH YOUR SENSES

Meats, fish, poultry, and plenty of other foods will cook differently at altitude. But the solution is as easy as using your senses (and an instant-read thermometer). Pay close attention to doneness indicators and less to recommended cooking times.

BRING THE RIGHT STOVE AND FUEL

The lower air pressure (and oxygen) at altitude can mess with some stoves' ability to combust. If you plan to spend time at altitude, check that your stove's manufacturer has optimized it to work at elevation.

And cold temperatures, which go hand in hand with altitude, can be a deal-killer for some types of camping fuel. See page 34 for more about what works best.

TWEAK YOUR BAKED GOODS

Altitudes above 3,000 feet change the way leavenings, like yeast, baking powder, baking soda, and acids, work; they also increase the rate at which baked goods evaporate liquids as they cook. To compensate, King Arthur Baking Company recommends the following:

→ Increasing oven temperatures by 15° to 25°F

→ Decreasing baking times by 5 to 8 minutes per recommended 30 minutes

→ Decreasing sugar by 1 tablespoon per 1 cup

→ Decreasing leavening amounts

→ Increasing liquids by 1 to 2 tablespoons at 3,000 feet, with an additional 1½ teaspoons per 1,000-foot increase

→ Adding an additional 1 tablespoon of flour at 3,500 feet, with another 1 tablespoon per each 1,500 feet after that

The King Arthur website has a detailed rundown if you've got a lot of high-altitude baking in your plans.

Ash-Burbled White Beans

with Chili-Parm Vinaigrette

Serves: 4 as a meal, or 6 as
a hearty side
Ingredient Weight: 26 ounces

I'll never not get a kick out of setting a pot of beans into a dying fire. That blazing heat soon turns into glowing coals, which smolder slowly as they transform into warm, insulating ashes. Beans cooked long and low in that environment come out perfectly intact but luxuriously creamy-centered, with a slow-food, fire-cooked flavor that no amount of in-town kitchen magic will ever match.

Now, how about a creamy, punchy, make-ahead chili-Parm vinaigrette to bathe them in? And a fistful of gorgeously earthy pickled collards to lend all that richness some crunch? This is one of those camp dishes your friends will never stop gushing about.

AT HOME

1 lemon, washed

One 1-ounce hunk Parmigiano-
 Reggiano cheese, very finely grated

3¼ teaspoons kosher salt

2 teaspoons chili flakes

6 tablespoons extra-virgin olive oil

Freshly ground black pepper

8 ounces collard greens

3 garlic cloves, smashed, peeled,
 and halved

½ cup red wine vinegar

¾ cup water

1 tablespoon granulated sugar

1 bay leaf

1. PREP THE CHILI-PARM VINAIGRETTE

In a medium bowl, use a Microplane grater to zest half of the lemon. Cut open the lemon and squeeze in the juice from both halves. Stir in the Parm, ¼ teaspoon of the salt, and the chili flakes, then drizzle in the olive oil while whisking the mixture to emulsify. (It'll be chunky!) Add a few solid cranks of pepper.

Pack the vinaigrette into a leakproof container and refrigerate or freeze. (It will keep for 1 month, frozen.)

2. PREP THE COLLARDS

Wash the collards, then, using a sharp knife, separate the tough stems from each leaf.

Stack the leaves and coarsely chop so the pieces are the size of dominoes. Trim and discard the bottoms of the stems, then chop the stems into ¼-inch rounds.

3. PICKLE AND PACK THE COLLARDS

In a small saucepan over medium-high, bring the garlic, vinegar, water, sugar, remaining 1 tablespoon salt, and bay leaf to a simmer.

Add the chopped collard stems, decrease the heat to low, then cover and simmer until the stems are tender-crunchy, about 10 minutes. Add the chopped collard leaves, loosely cover, and simmer for 10 to 15 minutes more, stirring occasionally, until the greens are slightly tender. Remove from the heat, discard the bay leaf and garlic, and let cool.

Transfer the pickled collards, along with enough liquid to cover, to a leakproof container or resealable bag, and refrigerate.

4. PREP THE FIRE; SORT THE BEANS

Let your fire burn down to a deep bed of glowing coals, with just a few active flames. Using a long stick or poker, clear a stable base for your pot. (It's best to go right down to ash or the ground.)

Dump the dried beans into a 3- or 4-quart, fire-safe saucepan with a lid. Pick through and discard any stones or broken or discolored beans. Add the garlic along with the herb sprigs.

AT CAMP

12 ounces dried white beans
(see Note)

3 garlic cloves, halved

A few sprigs mixed herbs (preferably
thyme, sage, and parsley)

Water for cooking the beans

2 teaspoons kosher salt

Prepared Chili-Parm Vinaigrette
(thawed) ❄

Prepared pickled collards, drained

A few nice hunks of crusty bread
(optional)

KEEPS

5 days, kept cold

5. START THE BEANS

Cover the beans with 3 inches of water, set the pan carefully into
your coals (fire gloves and a pot lifter are invaluable here), cover with
the lid, and mound the embers a short way up and around the pan.

Watch the saucepan closely during the first hour to ensure it
doesn't boil over. Ideally, it should come to a gentle simmer and no
more. If the heat seems too low, pack more embers around the pan
(but don't overdo it); if the pan gets too hot, pull some away.

6. SEASON AND TOP UP

After 90 minutes, top up the water as necessary. The beans should
be burbling gently. Season with the salt, cover, then mound gray
embers and ashes up the sides of the pan to gently heat and
insulate it.

When the beans have beautifully creamy centers but are still intact,
between 3 and 8 hours, remove the saucepan from the fire.

7. DRESS AND SERVE

Mince the remaining garlic clove and add to the vinaigrette.

Scoop and reserve ¼ cup of the beans' cooking water, then gently
drain (they're delicate!).

Dress the beans with the vinaigrette and gently stir in the collards.
Add a splash of the reserved cooking water to loosen as needed.
Serve immediately, along with the bread, if desired.

Notes

→ White kidney, cannellini, tarbais, cranberry, or any other creamy-
textured, mid-size bean variety, is ideal for this dish.

→ Dried beans are always best within a year of harvest. Buy yours
from a farmers' market, or a specialist brand, such as Rancho Gordo.

→ Don't be afraid to mix and match the different parts of this recipe.
The Chili-Parm Vinaigrette is a dream on fresh pasta, green beans,
broccoli, or rapini. The pickled collards go anywhere you need a pop
of freshness and crunch. As for the beans themselves, try dressing
them simply with oil and lemon juice.

Choose-Your-Own-Adventure Chicken Grill-Out

Serves: 4
Ingredient Weight: 38 ounces

These ready-to-grill chicken thighs begin with a creamy, sunshiny base of Dijon mustard, olive oil, lemon, and honey. But then depending on your mood, and your crowd, you can season them with either chopped fresh herbs (summery, fragrant, exquisite) or North Africa's brightly fiery harissa paste.

AT HOME

8 boneless chicken thighs (see Note)

Zest and juice of 1 lemon

Heaping 2 tablespoons Dijon mustard

4 teaspoons honey

5 tablespoons extra-virgin olive oil

1 teaspoon kosher salt

Adventure 1 Seasoning (Herbs)

Freshly ground black pepper

¼ cup chopped fresh rosemary

¼ cup chopped fresh thyme

½ cup coarsely chopped fresh parsley

Adventure 2 Seasoning (Harissa)

2 to 4 tablespoons harissa paste
  (see Note)

AT CAMP

Prepared chicken (thawed) ❄

KEEPS

2 days, after thawing, kept cold

1. MIX THE MARINADE AND FREEZE

In a large resealable freezer bag, combine the chicken thighs, lemon zest, lemon juice, mustard, honey, olive oil, salt, and your adventure seasoning of choice. Mix well to coat the chicken evenly.

Seal the bag and freeze. (The chicken will keep for 1 month, frozen.)

2. GRILL THE CHICKEN AND SERVE

Place a grill over medium-hot coals with direct and indirect cooking zones.

Grill the thighs until they're nicely browned, about 10 minutes, turning and relocating as necessary to avoid charring or flare-ups.

Move the thighs onto indirect heat and grill until the meat is cooked all the way through, the juices from the middle of the thighs run clear, and a thermometer stuck into the thickest part of a thigh reads 165°F, 10 to 20 minutes more. Serve immediately.

Notes

→ When it comes to chicken thighs, I will always belong to Camp Bone-Out, Skin-On. If you can't find thighs without bones, ask your butcher to bone them for you. And if you insist, meanwhile, on allying yourself with Camp Bone-Out, Skin-*Off*—or even Camp Chicken Breast way over at the marshy end of the lake—it's *your* adventure. Just be sure to use about 2 pounds of meat for the full recipe.

→ Harissa paste comes in myriad spice levels and flavor permutations. Taste it before you use it, so you know what you're dealing with.

Chimi-Spiked Flank Steak

Serves: 4
Ingredient Weight: 30 ounces

Chimichurri, the zingy South American herb sauce, plays double duty in this crowd-pleasing grill-up: as a slightly sweetened marinade for beef flank, and as a deliciously big-flavored finisher to serve on the side.

AT HOME

2 garlic cloves, coarsely chopped

2 teaspoons chili flakes

1 cup loosely packed fresh flat-leaf parsley leaves

½ cup loosely packed fresh cilantro leaves

⅓ cup loosely packed fresh oregano leaves

¼ cup red wine vinegar

½ cup extra-virgin olive oil

⅛ teaspoon kosher salt

1 tablespoon brown sugar

1½ pounds flank steak

AT CAMP

Marinated flank steak (thawed) ❄

Kosher or flaky salt

Prepared chimichurri sauce (thawed) ❄

KEEPS

The steak, 2 days, after thawing, kept cold; the chimichurri, 1 week, after thawing, kept cold

1. MAKE THE CHIMICHURRI

In a food processor, combine the garlic, chili flakes, parsley, cilantro, oregano, vinegar, olive oil, and salt and pulse to form a coarse sauce.

2. DIVIDE, MARINATE, AND PACK

Divide the chimichurri into two portions.

Pack one half into a leakproof container and freeze. This will be your sauce. (It will keep for 1 month, frozen.)

Add the brown sugar to the remaining half of the chimichurri and stir to make the marinade. In a resealable bag or container, combine the chimichurri with the flank steak, marinate in the refrigerator for 8 to 12 hours, and then freeze. (The steak will keep for 1 month, frozen.)

3. GRILL THE MEAT

Set a grill over high heat.

Remove the steak from the marinade and pat dry with paper towels. Put the steak on the grill and cook until it's nicely browned and cooked to no more than medium doneness, 3 to 5 minutes per side, or an instant-read thermometer registers 130°F. (Flank steak gets flubbery beyond that point.)

Transfer the steak to a warm plate or cutting board and let rest for 5 minutes.

4. CARVE AND SERVE

For tender meat, carve the steak thinly across the grain and on a bias (with your knife's edge at a slight forward angle). Arrange the steak slices on a platter, season liberally with salt, and serve with the chimichurri.

Campfire Paella Is the Best Paella

Serves: 4 to 6
Ingredient Weight: 3⅓ pounds

No other outdoors dish says *party* quite like paella. Paella is meant for feasts, for gatherings, for wood-fired cooking. And if you break it down into steps and pay attention as it cooks, truly great prep-ahead camp paella is remarkably straightforward.

While the main recipe is for the showstoppiest of showstoppers—fire-crisped rice under a tangle of squid and smoky seared shrimp—I've also included a chicken and artichoke version, as well as a vegan chickpea option. All three are celebrations in a pan, and absolutely sublime.

SPECIAL EQUIPMENT

13-inch paella pan or a large (12 inches or more) fireproof skillet

---

AT HOME

12 ounces cleaned squid, tubes (bodies) and tentacles

4 garlic cloves, peeled

2 medium yellow onions, coarsely chopped

1 red bell pepper, stemmed, seeded, and coarsely chopped

4 small ripe tomatoes

¼ cup extra-virgin olive oil

Kosher salt

½ teaspoon pimentón (Spanish smoked paprika)

½ pound green beans, trimmed

1. PREP THE SQUID

Coarsely chop half of the squid tubes and set aside for the sofrito.

Slice the remaining tubes into ¼-inch rings. (Leave the tentacles whole.) Pack the rings with the tentacles into a resealable bag, and freeze. (The squid will keep for 1 month, frozen.)

2. PREP THE SOFRITO

Put the garlic in a food processor and pulse to coarsely chop. Add the reserved chopped squid tubes, onions, and bell pepper and pulse to make a fine mixture. (Alternatively, finely chop the mixture with a sharp knife.)

Place a box grater over a medium bowl. Using the coarse side, grate the tomatoes. The pulp will fall into the bowl while the skin and stems (which you'll discard) stay in your hand. Set aside the tomato pulp.

3. SLOW-COOK THE SOFRITO

In a large skillet over medium heat, warm the olive oil. Add the onion-squid mixture and ½ teaspoon salt and cook, stirring frequently, until the liquid evaporates, about 10 minutes. Decrease the heat to medium-low and cook, stirring occasionally, until the mixture is tender, fragrant, and beginning to color, 5 to 10 minutes more.

Add the tomato pulp and pimentón to the skillet and cook for 10 minutes, stirring occasionally, until the sofrito is sizzling and the vegetables are richly brown in spots. Remove from the heat.

Let the sofrito cool and then seal it in a leakproof container or resealable bag and freeze. (It will keep for 1 month, frozen.)

4. PREP THE GREEN BEANS

Bring a medium pot of well-salted water to a boil over high heat. Add the green beans and let simmer until they're mellow-tasting and tender, 4 to 6 minutes.

Drain the beans, transfer to a clean kitchen towel, and let them cool and dry. Roll the beans in paper towels before packing in a resealable bag (see page 14).

CONTINUES →

AT CAMP

⅓ cup extra-virgin olive oil
(thawed) ❄

Prepared green beans

2 bunches green onions, trimmed of
roots and any mangled ends

Kosher salt

Prepared squid, patted dry
(thawed) ❄

½ pound raw wild shrimp or prawns
(thawed) ❄

Prepared sofrito (thawed) ❄

1½ cups paella rice (see Note)

1 teaspoon saffron threads

4½ cups water, plus ⅓ cup

½ teaspoon peperoncini piccanti
(optional; thawed) ❄

2 lemons, cut into halves

KEEPS

The raw chicken, shrimp, and squid,
2 days after thawing, kept cold; the
squid sofrito, 3 days after thawing,
kept cold; the sofrito without squid
and the chickpeas, 1 week, kept cold;
the green beans, 3 days, kept cold

5. BUILD THE RIGHT FIRE

The ideal paella fire has a deep bed of orange coals, with a few
small burning logs at its center and off to the side. It's medium-hot
when your cooking starts. But in the 30-odd minutes it'll take to
make the dish, the embers should fade to medium-low.

Place a sturdy grill 6 inches above the coal bed and make sure
it's level.

6. SEAR THE TOPPINGS

Place the paella pan on the grill and add 1 tablespoon of the olive
oil. The pan should be very hot and the oil should shimmer.

Add the green beans and green onions to the pan and sear, stirring
occasionally, until they char in spots, about 2 minutes. Adjust the
pan's position if it's too hot or cool. Remove the vegetables to
a clean plate, season with a large pinch of salt, and keep warm.

Add the squid to the pan, season with ¼ teaspoon salt, and sear
until it becomes browned and charry in spots, 2 to 3 minutes.
Remove to the vegetable plate and keep warm.

Add the shrimp to the pan, season with ¼ teaspoon salt, and
sear until it becomes pink and slightly charred in spots, around
2 minutes. Remove to the veg/squid plate and keep warm.

7. START THE RICE

Add the remaining ¼ cup olive oil and the sofrito to the pan and
cook, stirring frequently, until the sofrito is sizzling and fragrant,
about 2 minutes.

Add the rice and saffron to the pan and stir well to coat. Cook,
stirring frequently, until the grains turn translucent at their tips,
2 to 3 minutes.

Add the 4½ cups water, peperoncini piccanti (if using), and ½ teaspoon
salt to the pan, then stir once and give the pan a shake to distribute
the ingredients in an even layer.

8. LET IT COOK

Depending on your fire's heat, the paella will take 15 to 30 minutes
to finish cooking. Watch the pan closely and rotate or shift it on the
grill as needed so it's bubbling evenly, but do not stir.

Once most (but not all) of the liquid has cooked off, taste a few
grains of rice. They should be tender on their outsides but still
slightly firm in their centers. If the rice is still very firm, add up
to the remaining ⅓ cup water.

9. FINISH THE RICE

The final stage of cooking will require your senses. The sound will
progress from a busy burble (the residual liquid) to a snappy sizzle

(the olive oil) to a sizzle-crackle (the rice crust–forming stage). When the sizzle-crackling starts, arrange the seared vegetables, squid, and shrimp on top of the rice. Give your paella a few additional minutes, using your eyes and nose (or a look under the rice with the tip of a spoon) to ensure it doesn't burn. If you like a crisp, golden crust where the rice touches the pan, this is the stage to be brave.

Remove the pan from the heat, cover with aluminum foil or a clean kitchen towel, and let the paella rest for 5 minutes.

10. GRILL THE LEMONS AND SERVE

As the paella rests, grill the lemon halves, cut-side down.

Serve the paella with the grilled lemons.

CHICKEN AND ARTICHOKE VARIATION

Ingredient Weight: 3¾ pounds

Omit the squid, shrimp, and saffron.

In At Camp, Step 2, after searing the vegetables, season **1 pound of boneless, skinless chicken thighs (thawed)** ❄ with ½ **teaspoon salt**. Add the remaining olive oil to the pan and sear the thighs until they're well-browned all over, about 5 minutes. Remove to a clean plate and keep warm.

Add **8 ounces oil- or water-packed artichokes (drained and quartered)** to the pan and sear until they're warm and gently turn color, about 3 minutes. Remove to the plate with the chicken and keep warm.

In At Camp, Step 3, after adding the water to the pan, snug the chicken thighs and artichokes into the rice. Continue as directed.

CHICKPEA VARIATION

Ingredient Weight: 3 pounds

Omit the squid and shrimp.

In At Home, Step 3, **double the pimentón to 1 teaspoon**.

In At Camp, Step 3, after adding the remaining olive oil, add **one 15-ounce can chickpeas (drained and rinsed)** ❄ to the pan and sear, stirring frequently, for 3 minutes, before adding the sofrito.

In At Camp, Step 3, while adding the water to the rice, **increase the salt to ¾ teaspoon**. Continue as directed.

Note

→ Use a short-grained rice variety specifically suited for paella (such as bomba, bahia, Calasparra, or senia) or a risotto rice, like carnaroli or Arborio.

RIB NIGHT

Full-on grilled sparerib dinner at camp with all the fixings? Easy when you do most of it ahead.

The ribs in this showstopper meal get braised at home with exactly three ingredients: lemons (so many lemons!), salt, and bottled sauce. (Look for bottled sauces with vinegar and molasses high in the ingredients list; Stubb's Original Bar-B-Q is a great choice.) They freeze with ease, then sizzle and sweeten under a sticky glaze as you reheat them over the fire, cooking up succulent, fall-apart tender, and sublimely sweet-and-sour. Alongside vinegary-porky premade collard greens and freshly grilled corn, this fuss-free rib fest is one of summer eating's greatest joys.

Fire-Grilled Corn

Serves: 4 as a side
Ingredient Weight: 4 pounds

AT CAMP

4 ears corn, in husks

4 tablespoons salted butter
   (thawed) ❄

Kosher salt

KEEPS

The corn lasts several days
unrefrigerated, but will be at its best
for no more than 3 days, kept cold

1. GRILL AND SERVE

Lay the unhusked corn at the edge of a fire or on a medium-hot grill
and roast, turning as needed, until the husks are darkly colored and
the kernels feel tender, 15 to 20 minutes.

Husk the corn and serve with the butter and salt.

Beer and Bacon Collard Greens

AT HOME

1½ pounds collard greens, rinsed

4 slices thick-cut bacon, cut into ¼-inch pieces

1 tablespoon salted butter

2 garlic cloves, minced

One 12-ounce bottle lager beer

1 cup water

¼ cup apple cider vinegar

¼ cup packed Demerara sugar or dark brown sugar

1 teaspoon kosher salt

½ teaspoon chili flakes

1 teaspoon mustard seeds

AT CAMP

Prepared collard greens (thawed) ❄

1 tablespoon salted butter (thawed) ❄

KEEPS

5 days, after thawing, kept cold

1. PREP THE GREENS

Tear or cut the collard leaves from their stems and discard the stems.

Stack the leaves and cut into roughly 1 by 2-inch pieces.

2. COOK THE FLAVOR BASE

In a medium, heavy saucepan over medium heat, cook the bacon until it's rendered much of its fat and is beginning to brown, 8 to 12 minutes.

Drain and discard all but 2 tablespoons of the bacon fat, add the butter and garlic to the pan, and cook, stirring frequently, until the garlic is soft and fragrant, about 2 minutes.

3. WILT THE COLLARDS AND SEASON

In two batches, add the collards to the pan, tossing and stirring the first addition to wilt in the bacon mixture for 1 minute before adding the rest. Add the beer, water, vinegar, sugar, salt, and chili flakes and stir to combine, pressing the collards under the liquid.

Meanwhile, in a small skillet over medium heat, toast the mustard seeds until they begin to color and pop, 1 to 2 minutes.

Add the mustard seeds to the collards and stir the mixture well, pressing the leaves into the liquid.

4. COOK, COOL, AND PACK

Decrease the heat to medium-low and loosely cover the pan so steam can escape. Cook, stirring occasionally, until the collards are tender and the liquid has reduced by half, about 90 minutes.

Remove the lid, increase the heat to medium-high, and let simmer, stirring occasionally, until just a few tablespoons of the cooking liquid remain at the bottom of the pan. Remove from the heat.

Let the collards cool, then pack tightly into a resealable freezer bag or leakproof container and freeze. (They will keep for 1 month, frozen.)

5. HEAT AND SERVE

Put the collards in a medium saucepan over medium heat and warm to a simmer. Stir in the butter before serving.

Sweet-Tangy
Lemon Ribs

Serves: 4 to 6
Ingredient Weight: 5 pounds

AT HOME

6 lemons, washed

5 pounds spareribs (aka "side ribs")
or St. Louis–style ribs

1 tablespoon kosher salt

10 ounces bottled barbecue sauce

Freshly ground black pepper

1½ cups hot water

AT CAMP

2 tablespoons vegetable oil

Prepared ribs (thawed) ❄

10 ounces bottled barbecue sauce

2 lemons

Kosher salt

KEEPS

3 days, after thawing, kept cold

1. LAYER IN THE LEMONS AND RIBS

Preheat the oven to 350°F.

Cut each lemon into ¼-inch slices. Distribute two-thirds of the lemon slices evenly on the bottom of a large roasting pan.

Season the ribs with the salt, then coat them with the barbecue sauce.

Snug the ribs in a single layer over the lemon slices. (Some minor overlapping isn't the end of the world.) Top with the remaining lemon slices and season well with pepper.

2. COVER AND BRAISE

Add the hot water to the pan and cover tightly with aluminum foil.

Bake the ribs until the meat is tender and beginning to pull away from the bones, about 2 hours. Remove from the oven.

3. PACK AND FREEZE

Let the ribs cool, drain, and discard the lemon slices. Pack in a large resealable bag and freeze. (They will keep for 1 month, frozen.)

4. READY A FIRE

Prepare a medium-hot fire for grilling with direct and indirect cooking zones. Set a grill 6 to 8 inches above the coals, then clean the grate and brush or wipe it well with the vegetable oil.

5. GRILL THE RIBS

Lay the ribs over direct heat and brush their tops generously with the sauce. Turn the ribs every few minutes to heat and brown them, about 10 minutes total. Brush each side generously with the sauce when it faces up.

6. SERVE

When the ribs are nearly ready, halve the lemons and place them over direct heat, cut-side down, to caramelize, about 5 minutes. Cut the meat into individual ribs and season with salt.

Serve the ribs with the grilled lemons, collards, and corn.

KEBAB PARTY

This three-part showstopper dinner, built around smoky, juicy, spice-kissed lamb kebabs; puffy, fresh-baked chapatis; and an extraordinarily tasty sweet-sour salad, is to my mind, one of the single greatest uses of a glowing campfire.

The kebabs, a staple food around northwest China's Xinjiang region, get earthy depth from a blizzard of cumin and deliciously mouth-tingling brightness from Sichuan peppercorns. Better still, they're fully prepped at home and frozen on wooden skewers. All you need to do is throw them on the grill.

As for the salad, adapted from Northwest Chinese food expert Wei Guo's superb blog, *Red House Spice*, it takes zero prep and no refrigeration. Combine the onion, vinegar, sugar, and salt in a bowl and you have a tasty garnish; build it out with the remaining ingredients and it'll become a fixture in your outdoor feasts.

The chapati—the most versatile flatbreads you'll ever make—also come ready-to-cook. They puff up with steam over your fire or camp stove like magically delicious little dirigibles. That never gets old. (For a lighter-weight, long-storing, no-refrigeration-required option, prep and pack the flour-salt mix at home, then mix and form your breads at camp.)

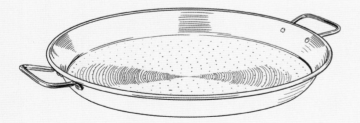

Puff-and-Serve Chapati

Makes: 12 chapati
Ingredient Weight: 18 ounces
  (prepped and frozen);
  10 ounces (dry mix only)

AT HOME

2½ cups atta (see Note) or whole-
  wheat flour, plus more as needed

1¼ teaspoons kosher salt

2¼ cups warm water, plus more
  as needed

AT CAMP

Prepared chapati (thawed) ❄

KEEPS

The chapati, 1 day, after thawing,
kept cold; the dry mix, 1 month,
unrefrigerated

1. MIX AND FORM THE DOUGH

In a medium bowl, combine 2 cups of the atta and the salt and stir to mix.

In three equal additions, pour in the water, mixing and moistening the flour with the fingers of one hand between pours.

Work the mixture with your hand until it forms a ball, then knead it in the bowl for 1 minute. If the dough feels dry and stiff, add ½ teaspoon warm water at a time until it's supple; if it's too wet, add 1 to 2 teaspoons flour. You want the dough to be tacky, but not sticky; you should be able to knead it without clumps breaking away in your hands.

2. KNEAD AND REST THE DOUGH

Lightly flour a clean work surface (a cutting board or skillet is great if you're doing this at camp) and knead the dough for 6 to 10 minutes, smooshing it down and away with your palm and folding it over itself in a frenetic—or Zenned-out; you are how you knead, really—CPR-like loop. You're done when the ball is Play-Doh smooth and holds the impression of a finger poke.

Cover the ball with a clean, damp cloth or paper towel and let it rest for 20 to 30 minutes. (When I'm camping, I'll sometimes put the ball back into a resealable bag and throw it somewhere warm.) This resting stage helps ensure tender breads.

3. ROLL THE BREADS

Transfer the dough ball back to the floured work surface, press into an even round, and then cut it, like a pizza, into twelve equal pieces. Roll each piece into a ball, toss them back into your mixing bowl with the remaining ½ cup flour, and cover.

Working one at a time, put a dough ball on the floured work surface and flatten with your hands to form a fat disc, then use a rolling pin or water bottle to smooth each disc into a round, rotating the dough as you work. Toss a little flour under and over the rounds as you go to prevent sticking. They'll be between 5 and 7 inches in diameter once you're done.

4. PACK AND FREEZE

Flour each finished disc well on both sides, place on a small sheet of parchment paper, and then stack them, making sure each one is separated by the paper. Wrap the stack tightly with aluminum foil, pack into a resealable bag or airtight container, and freeze. (It will keep for 1 month, frozen.)

5. COOK THE BREADS AND SERVE

In a large, dry skillet over medium-high heat, cook the chapatis one or two at a time. Cook the first side for 30 to 60 seconds, until the top begins to form dime-size bubbles. Using tongs, flip the chapati and cook for another 30 seconds or so.

Flip the chapati one last time; if your heat source is a fire or camp stove, flip it directly onto the grill or grate. It should inflate almost immediately into a ball. Let it blister lightly, 10 to 20 seconds, turning as needed for even cooking. Serve warm.

Notes

→ Atta flour is a finely stone-ground, high-gluten flour; although whole-wheat flour will also work well here, it's worth seeking out atta for its distinctive texture and flavor. You'll find it at South Asian, East African, and many Caribbean grocers, if not at your local supermarket. It's also available online.

→ Many chapati recipes don't include salt; the amount in this recipe brings out the bread's flavor without overwhelming it, but don't hesitate to dial it back, especially if you plan to serve the breads with high-sodium curries or meats.

→ You can also form the chapati the old-school way by slapping the dough discs hard between your palms until they're the proper thinness. It's a bit more work than rolling, and the final product will cook up more rustic, but they're tasty nonetheless.

Sizzling Cumin Lamb Kebabs

Serves: 4
Ingredient Weight: 1½ pounds

AT HOME

1 tablespoon whole Sichuan
   peppercorns

2 tablespoons whole cumin seeds

2 teaspoons chili flakes

2 teaspoons kosher salt

1 garlic clove, finely chopped

2 tablespoons vegetable oil

1½ pounds boneless lamb leg or
   shoulder, plus an ounce or two
   of additional fat

AT CAMP

Prepared lamb kebabs (thawed) ❄

Prepared spice mix

KEEPS

2 days, after thawing, kept cold

1. SOAK THE SKEWERS; TOAST THE SPICES

Soak ten wooden skewers in water for 30 minutes.

Meanwhile, in a dry skillet over medium heat, combine the peppercorns and cumin seeds and toast, stirring frequently, until the cumin is slightly colored and the mixture is intensely aromatic, about 2 minutes.

2. GRIND THE SPICE MIX AND PACK

Transfer the toasted spices and the chili flakes to a spice mill, mortar, or resealable bag. Grind or crush with a heavy object to make a very coarse powder. Add the salt.

Pack half of the spice mix in a resealable bag or container. (It will keep for 1 month, unrefrigerated.) Reserve the second half for the next step.

3. CUT THE LAMB AND MARINATE

In a medium bowl, combine the garlic, vegetable oil, and reserved spice mix and stir well.

Cut the lamb into 1-inch cubes. Slice the additional fat into 1-inch squares about ⅛ inch thick. Add the lamb and fat to the garlic-oil mixture and stir to coat well.

4. SKEWER, FREEZE, AND PACK

Line a baking sheet with parchment paper. Thread the meat and fat, alternating the pieces, onto the prepared skewers. Be sure to leave a bit of space between each piece so they can char-grill all around. Lay the skewers on the prepared baking sheet and freeze overnight.

Once the skewers are frozen solid, trim and discard the sharp ends, wrap tightly with the parchment paper and then a piece of aluminum foil, taking care that the skewers don't poke through.

Transfer the kebabs to a resealable bag, expel the air, seal, and freeze. (They will keep for 1 month, frozen.)

5. GRILL THE KEBABS AND SERVE

Prepare a deep bed of high-heat coals with direct and indirect grilling areas. Place the grill 3 to 5 inches above the coals.

Place the kebabs on the grill and cook, turning frequently but allowing them to char, spit, and flare up occasionally. Dust them with the reserved spice mix as they cook. (If you've got quick hands, make all the kebabs at once; for a more relaxed experience, do them in a few batches.) Jockey them between direct and indirect heat if the flare-ups become constant. Your goal is sizzling, dark-grilled, spice-flecked meat that's cooked to medium in the middle, 4 to 6 minutes.

Serve the kebabs with the sweet-and-sour salad and chapati.

Note

→ The secret to making these kebabs juicy and irresistible is using plenty of lamb fat. Ask your butcher to leave a generous cap of fat on the meat, and preferably to slip you a little extra too. As the kebabs grill over super-hot coals, this fat melts and sizzles, basting the meat and amplifying the flavor of the spice. And if all that fat makes you clutch your chest, don't worry—most of it just drips into the fire.

Simply Sweet-and-Sour Salad

Serves: 4 as a garnish or side
Ingredient Weight: 9½ ounces

AT CAMP

½ medium red onion, thinly sliced

1 tablespoon Chinkiang vinegar (see Note)

⅛ teaspoon granulated sugar

⅛ teaspoon kosher salt

1 handful cherry tomatoes, halved (optional)

1 jalapeño or other hot green chili, stemmed, seeded, and sliced (optional)

10 cilantro sprigs, chopped (optional)

1. TOSS AND SERVE

In a large bowl, toss together the onion, vinegar, sugar, and salt. Let stand for 10 minutes to marinate.

Add the tomatoes, jalapeño, and cilantro, if desired. Correct the seasoning as needed before serving.

Note

→ Made from fermented black sticky rice, Chinkiang vinegar, also known as "Chinese black vinegar," brings rich, sophisticated depth and tartness. (It's also a key ingredient in the dan dan noodle sauce on page 205.) You can find Chinkiang vinegar at Chinese grocers, if not at your local supermarket.

KEEPS

1 week, unrefrigerated; with optional additions, up to 5 days, unrefrigerated

STEAKHOUSE

Maybe you know a steakhouse where they grill 2½-pound, dry-aged, bone-in ribeye steaks over real wood embers until they're buttery and juicy and crisply fire-crusted, cooked perfectly to medium-rare. Where the potatoes are rubbed in olive oil and salt, then roasted slowly in the fire's ashes so their brittle skins come out absurdly potato-y and their insides arrive nearly as fluffy as mashed. Where they serve pots of creamed spinach that tastes prodigally rich and delicious. And where they dish it up under a wide-open sky. That's the steakhouse of my dreams. And in truth, I've never found one—at least not one that wasn't out in the wild.

The ribeye in this showstopper has a dark, sizzling, beautifully seasoned crust and a perfectly pink interior. The trick, if you can call it that, is shuttling your steak back and forth between intense, crust-forming heat (aka the obscenely hot side of your grill) and resting heat (the indirect side), so the middle has enough time to catch up.

If you've always felt intimidated by thick, bone-in steaks, this recipe might just change your life.

This sort of grilling takes a bit of patience; your total cook time, plus a rest at the end, will stretch to somewhere between 40 and 55 minutes for medium-rare meat. But the payoff is a juicy, meltingly tender texture, and the sort of fire-grilled, wild-cooked flavor even the best steakhouses can only dream about. The spinach and potatoes, meanwhile, are every bit the ribeye's equal.

Really Creamy Spinach

AT HOME

Two 10-ounce blocks chopped
    frozen spinach

3 tablespoons salted butter

2 medium shallots, thinly sliced

2 garlic cloves, minced

1¼ teaspoons kosher salt

3 tablespoons all-purpose flour

½ cup heavy cream

1½ cups milk

⅛ teaspoon freshly grated nutmeg

Freshly ground black pepper

AT CAMP

Prepared creamed spinach
    (thawed) ❄

2 tablespoons salted butter
    (thawed) ❄

2 tablespoons water

Juice of ½ lemon

Kosher salt and freshly ground
    black pepper

KEEPS

2 days, after thawing, kept cold

1. THAW AND DRAIN THE SPINACH

Thaw the spinach according to the package instructions. Drain as much liquid as possible from the spinach. (Wet spinach equals insipid-tasting spinach.) Squeeze it in a potato ricer if you have one, or gather it up inside a clean kitchen towel and then squeeze the towel over a bowl or sink until your neck veins pop out. Set aside.

2. BUILD THE SAUCE

In a medium skillet or saucepan over medium-low heat, melt the butter. Add the shallots, garlic, and ¼ teaspoon of the salt and cook, stirring occasionally, until the shallots and garlic are very soft and fragrant and just beginning to turn a light golden brown, 5 to 10 minutes.

Add the flour to the skillet and cook, whisking the mixture until it turns light blond, about 2 minutes. In a thin stream, slowly add the cream, whisking to incorporate. Pour in the milk, increase the heat to medium, bring this sauce to a simmer, and cook, whisking frequently, until it thickens, 1 to 2 minutes.

3. PUT THEM TOGETHER

Add the chopped spinach, nutmeg, remaining 1 teaspoon salt and ten good cranks of pepper to the skillet and cook, stirring frequently, until the mixture is bubbling and the spinach has relaxed into the sauce, about 3 minutes.

Remove the spinach from the heat. Let it cool, then pack it in a resealable bag and freeze. (It will keep for 1 month, frozen.)

4. HEAT AND SERVE

In a small saucepan or skillet over low heat, combine the creamed spinach, butter, and water, and warm through. Season with the lemon juice, salt, and pepper before serving.

Ash-Baked Potatoes

Serves: 4 as a side
Ingredient Weight: 3 pounds

AT HOME

4 large russet potatoes

1 tablespoon extra-virgin olive oil

2 teaspoons kosher salt

AT CAMP

Prepared potatoes

4 tablespoons salted butter (thawed) ❄

1 bunch green onions, trimmed and thinly sliced

Sour cream for serving (optional)

KEEPS

The uncooked, wrapped potatoes, 5 days, kept cold.

1. PREP THE POTATOES

Scrub the potatoes and trim away any eyes or major blemishes.

2. SEASON AND WRAP

Cut out and lay four 10 by 18-inch pieces of heavy-duty aluminum foil on your counter.

Rub the potatoes all over with the olive oil and salt, wrap each one tightly in the foil, and then refrigerate.

3. ROAST THE POTATOES

Snug the potatoes right up to the edge of a hot coal bed, then mound ashes and gray embers all around but not over them. Cook for 40 to 70 minutes, turning every 10 minutes, until they're soft when you squeeze them and tender all the way through when pierced with a fork.

For crisp, blistered skins and light, fluffy interiors, finish the wrapped potatoes with a final 10 to 15 minutes directly on or in the hot, orange embers. This is a medium-risk/high-reward wild cooking moment, so watch them closely for signs (or smells) of burning, and don't be afraid to pull one off the fire and peek inside.

4. DRESS AND SERVE

Unwrap the potatoes and serve with the butter, green onions, and sour cream, if desired.

Note

→ For food safety reasons, if you're keeping leftovers, be sure to remove the potatoes from the foil, let them cool, and keep them cold.

Perfect Fire-Grilled Ribeye Steak

Serves: 4
Ingredient Weight: 43 ounces

SPECIAL EQUIPMENT

An instant-read thermometer (optional but highly recommended)

AT HOME

2 tablespoons unsalted butter, at room temperature

½ teaspoon Worcestershire sauce

½ teaspoon chopped fresh thyme

Freshly ground black pepper

AT CAMP

One 2½-pound bone-in ribeye steak (aka cowboy steak; see Note), cut 2½ inches thick (thawed) ❄

1 tablespoon kosher salt

1 tablespoon vegetable oil

Prepared Worcestershire butter (thawed) ❄

Maldon or other flaky sea salt

KEEPS

The steak, 3 days, after thawing, kept cold; the compound butter, 1 week, after thawing, kept cold

1. MAKE THE WORCESTERSHIRE BUTTER

In a small bowl, combine the butter, Worcestershire, and thyme and mix with a fork until thoroughly incorporated. Season with fifteen to twenty good cranks of pepper.

Transfer the mixture onto a piece of parchment paper, wax paper, or plastic wrap; roll it into a short, tidy cylinder; and refrigerate or freeze. (It'll keep 1 month, frozen.)

2. SEASON YOUR STEAK

About 2 hours before you want to eat, unwrap the steak, pat it dry with paper towels, and then season it with the kosher salt, sprinkling from above and turning it so every bit of its surface (top, bottom, and sides) is heavily coated. Using your hands, press the salt into the meat. Yes, that *is* a lot of salt. But no, your steak will not be oversalted. I promise.

Let the seasoned steak rest at air temperature.

3. PREPARE YOUR FIRE

Prepare a two-zone fire, with one side very hot and the other indirect. You'll need a lot of coals to do this right, plus a few burning logs off to the side, to replenish your coal supply as required.

Place the grill 3 or 4 inches above the coal bed. Clean your grate, and brush or wipe it with vegetable oil.

4. GRILL, REST, FLIP, REPEAT

Place the steak on the hottest part of the grill and sear for 3 minutes per side, so it's nicely colored. Flip the steak onto indirect heat so the rib bone is closest to the high-heat coals but not over them.

Rest the steak over indirect heat for 5 minutes, then repeat the sear-rest routine, sliding the steak to direct heat to sear and color on one side for 3 minutes, then flipping it to indirect heat for 5 minutes more. Your steak will take between 30 and 40 minutes of that sear-rest grilling for medium-rare doneness, and slightly longer for medium.

5. REMOVE FROM THE HEAT AND REST

Once the steak reaches 125°F in its center (for medium-rare) or 130°F (for medium), transfer to a clean, warm plate, and gently rub the meat all over with half of the Worcestershire butter.

Let the meat rest for 10 to 15 minutes; the internal temperature will rise another 10°F.

Add a few small pieces of wood to your fire to raise it to maximum temperature for a final sear.

6. SEAR AGAIN, SLICE, AND SERVE

Return the steak to the hottest part of your grill and sear for 45 seconds per side to get it sizzling again. Remove the steak from the heat and rub it all over with the remaining compound butter.

Cut away the bone and place it at the center of a serving plate, then slice the meat and arrange the slices around the bone. Season with flaky salt.

Serve the steak immediately, with the creamed spinach and baked potatoes.

Notes

→ If your butcher sells dry-aged steak, I highly recommend it. The flavor's deeper, richer, and more concentrated steaky, and the aging makes the meat more tender too. It'll be pricey, yes, but nothing compared to what you'd pay at a steakhouse.

→ Provided you're cooking over glowing coals or embers, flare-ups are nothing to be alarmed about, especially at the start of grilling. If you're getting them persistently after 15 minutes or so, adjust your fire or reposition your grill to limit them; short and infrequent flare-ups are good, but constant flare-ups are not.

→ If it's very cold or windy, tent the steak with aluminum foil to retain a bit of heat as it rests on the grill and after cooking.

MORNINGS AFTER

I am not, in my normal life, a breakfast person.

I'll have it, sure—if it doesn't take much doing. Granola: Fine. French toast? Get real. But being outside, fresh air and all that, triggers whatever latent, breakfast-loving side my city life ordinarily suppresses. Give me torrents of maple syrup on buttermilk pancakes, and if I'm out in the wild, I'm jelly, basically. Say the words "black bean chilaquiles" as I step out of my tent, and I guess I'll be eating for three.

You'll find just those sorts of breakfasts in the following pages, as well as what breakfast people might more properly consider brunch. There are quick, convenient (and very delicious) overnight oats, as well as killer granola that's actually a pleasure to bake at home. There are eggs soft-roasted in warm, deep ashes (yep, it is a terrific party trick), and monumentally satisfying (really!) corn and green onion skillet cakes gone crisp at their edges with caramelized cheese. There's also a useful guide to making truly great coffee in the wild. If you're a breakfast-cocktail person, you're covered too. With the help of a little bottle of premade batter, there's even French toast, and it's great enough that it could almost make me a breakfast person back in town.

Gin Caesar Slushies

Serves: 4
Ingredient Weight: 2¾ pounds,
plus optional garnishes

Think of these gin-based Caesars as the Bloody Mary's brash northern cousin. They're spicy, savory, and ridiculously refreshing, with a welcome aromatic top note from the gin. Thanks to all their vegetable content, they're even *almost* healthful, too, brilliant served with breakfast in the wild.

AT HOME

1 cup water

20 ounces Clamato cocktail juice

8 ounces gin

4 ounces jalapeño brine (from a jar of pickled jalapeños)

4 teaspoons fresh lemon juice

1 teaspoon Worcestershire sauce

8 dashes Tabasco sauce

1 teaspoon freshly ground black pepper

¼ teaspoon kosher salt

AT CAMP

Prepared Caesar mix (partially thawed) ❄

Celery sticks, olives, pickled beans, lemon wedges, and other garnishes for serving

KEEPS

5 days, after thawing, kept cold, or 2 weeks, frozen

1. MIX, PACK, AND FREEZE THE CAESAR MIX

In a 1.5-liter soda bottle, combine the water, Clamato, gin, jalapeño brine, lemon juice, Worcestershire, Tabasco, pepper, and salt. Shake well and freeze for 24 hours.

2. SHAKE, POUR, AND GARNISH

Shake the slushy Caesar mix well to break up its ice, pour into tall glasses (or crappy camping mugs), and garnish as desired. Serve immediately.

Notes

→ These are meant to be imbibed as slushies; if you'd rather drink them on ice, omit the water from the recipe.

→ If you'd like a vegan version, or you're really not into seafood in your cocktails—the drink's base mixer is Clamato juice—turn this into a Red Snapper (that's a Bloody Mary but made with gin) by swapping the Clamato for straight tomato juice.

Corn, Cheddar, and Green Onion Skillet Cakes

Serves: 4 to 6
Ingredient Weight: 28 ounces

These crispy buttermilk-and-cornmeal skillet cakes pop with juicy corn kernels, and crunch at their edges with bits of pan-caramelized cheddar cheese.

AT HOME

1 cup all-purpose flour

1 cup cornmeal

¼ cup buttermilk powder

¼ cup granulated sugar

¼ cup chia seeds or ground flaxseed

4 teaspoons baking powder

¾ teaspoon kosher salt

1½ cups finely grated cheddar cheese

AT CAMP

12 ounces maple-flavored breakfast sausages (optional; thawed) ❄

Prepared dry mix ❄

2 cups water

10 green onions, sliced

1 cup corn kernels, fresh or frozen (thawed) ❄

3 tablespoons salted butter (thawed) ❄

¼ cup pure maple syrup (thawed) ❄

KEEPS

The corn kernels and sausages, 3 days, after thawing, kept cold; the dry mix, 5 days, unrefrigerated, or 2 weeks, kept cold

1. MIX AND PACK

In a resealable bag or container, combine the flour, cornmeal, buttermilk powder, sugar, chia seeds, baking powder, salt, and cheddar, making sure to toss the cheese well in the mixture to coat. Refrigerate or freeze. (It will keep for 2 months, frozen.)

2. COOK THE SAUSAGES (IF USING)

In a medium, nonstick skillet over medium heat, fry the sausages until they're well-browned and cooked through. Transfer to a plate and cover to keep warm.

3. MIX THE BATTER

Meanwhile, in a medium bowl (or other batter-worthy vessel), combine the dry mix and water. Stir to incorporate but don't overmix. Add the green onions and corn, fold them in, and let this batter rest for 5 minutes to thicken.

4. COOK THE SKILLET CAKES

Wipe out the skillet and set over medium heat. When a drop of water splashed into the pan dances for a second or two and then evaporates, it's ready. Add ½ tablespoon of the butter to coat the pan, then pour (or plop) in ¾ cup of the batter. Shake the pan to spread the batter around a bit; this will get you caramelized edges.

Cook the skillet cake, undisturbed, until bubbles form and burst in the middle, leaving open holes behind, 2 to 4 minutes. Carefully flip the cake, then add a few of the cooked sausages to the edge of the pan to reheat. Cook another few minutes, until the cake is dark at its edges, its underside turns golden, and it's cooked through. Repeat with the remaining butter, batter, and sausages.

5. SERVE

Serve the skillet cakes warm with the sausages and maple syrup.

Ash-Roasted Eggs

with Grilled Toast and Good Honey

Serves: 4
Ingredient Weight: 31 ounces

I feel safe in calling this the most low-fi camp recipe you'll make this year. Ash-roasted eggs, done right, are rich, soft, and just the slightest bit campfire-smoky. The simple technique for making them dates back to the Romans, at least. The dish also sounds, to the unfamiliar, like some kind of prank.

Which makes them that much more delicious when you open them up, with the whites just set and the yolks the color of marmalade. Alongside warm grilled bread and flavorful honey, this basic breakfast stops time with every bite.

AT CAMP

8 large eggs (see Note)

8 thick slices sourdough bread

4 tablespoons salted butter
(thawed) ❄

⅓ cup raw, local, flavorful honey
(thawed) ❄

Kosher or flaky salt

KEEPS

See Note

1. PREPARE YOUR FIRE

Pull warm, deep ashes and smoldering gray embers from a dying fire, or light a hot, fast fire of twigs and sticks in an existing fire pit and let it burn until it's nearly out.

2. ROAST THE EGGS

One at a time, stand each egg upright and use the point of a sharp knife to carefully tap a hole at its peak; the hole should be about as wide as a spaghetti strand. This will keep your egg from exploding in the heat.

Nestle each egg into the ash bed so the hole is facing up, then gently mound it with ashes and embers to three-fourths of the way up. If your ashes are very hot, the eggs may push some of their whites out of the steam holes; this is normal. If it happens, gently scrape the whites away so the holes remain clear. If it's cold out, you can mound the ashes nearly up to the top of the eggs.

The eggs should be soft-cooked in about 7 minutes, or hard-cooked in 10 minutes. But this is primitive cooking, not the Modernist Cuisine research lab. I wouldn't bet my breakfast on cooking these by the clock.

3. GRILL THE BREAD

While the eggs are cooking, toast the bread slices on a grill over the glowing coals, 1 to 2 minutes per side. If you don't have a grill, lean the slices at the edge of the fire.

Remove the bread from the heat, butter generously from edge to edge (don't scrimp at the edges!), and cover to keep warm.

4. SERVE

Using a fire glove or tongs, remove an egg from the ashes, then crack its top open as you would a soft-boiled egg to see if the whites are set to your taste. (If it's underdone, replace the top and carefully stick it back into the ashes.) When the eggs are ready, open the remaining ones and serve with the buttered toast drizzled with the honey and salt alongside.

Note

→ Freshly laid eggs have a natural bacteria-blocking barrier on their shells that makes them safe to store unrefrigerated. In North America, however, most eggs must be washed before they're sold; the washing removes that barrier. So, if you're lucky enough to have access to unwashed eggs fresh from a farm, you can store them without refrigeration for 2 weeks. If you get them from the supermarket, it's best to keep them in a cooler and eat them before their best-by date. (For packing tips, see "Of Course You Can Bring Eggs!" on page 15.)

Buttermilk Powder Pancakes

Serves: 4
Ingredient Weight: 18 ounces

These golden, fluffy, just-add-water pancakes use buttermilk powder to leaven and tenderize as their batter cooks—and for its homestyle, real buttermilk tang. And in place of eggs, they use your choice of flaxseed meal (so healthy!) or chia seeds (aka Hippie Sprinkles). So you can feel good about what you're eating on the trail. The simple mix takes less than five minutes to make and lasts a month (or more) in a pack. And it cooks up just as easily as the boxed stuff from the store.

AT HOME

2 cups all-purpose flour

4 teaspoons baking powder

½ teaspoon kosher salt

¼ cup chia seeds or ground flaxseed

¼ cup buttermilk powder (see Note)

¼ cup granulated sugar

AT CAMP

Prepared pancake mix

2 cups water

3 tablespoons salted butter or vegetable oil, plus more butter for serving (thawed) ❄

2 ounces pure maple syrup (thawed) ❄

KEEPS

The dry mix, 1 month, unrefrigerated; the syrup, up to 3 days, unrefrigerated, or indefinitely, kept cold

1. MIX AND PACK

In a resealable bag or container, combine the flour, baking powder, salt, chia seeds, buttermilk powder, and sugar. Seal the bag and shake well to incorporate the pancake mix.

2. MAKE THE BATTER

In a medium bowl, combine the pancake mix and water and stir to incorporate. Don't overmix; a few lumps in pancake batter are a good thing—it means you'll have tender, fluffy pancakes.

3. COOK THE PANCAKES AND SERVE

Set a wide, heavy skillet over medium heat. When a drop of water splashed onto its surface sizzles before evaporating, it's ready. Grease the pan with 1 teaspoon of the butter, then pour in the batter (¼ cup for small pancakes, or ¾ cup to make pan-size flapjacks).

Cook the pancakes, undisturbed, until bubbles form and burst in their middles, leaving open holes behind, 1 to 3 minutes. Flip the pancakes, then cook for another few minutes, until they're golden on their undersides and cooked through. Transfer to a plate.

Wipe down the skillet, add another 1 teaspoon butter, and repeat with the remaining batter. (If using oil, add more as needed.)

Serve the pancakes, warm, with butter and maple syrup.

Notes

→ Buttermilk powder is often sold in supermarket baking sections. If you can't get it there, it's easy to find at bulk foods stores and online.

→ If you'd like to add fresh berries or chopped fruit, scatter a total of 1 cup per recipe over the uncooked pancakes after you pour the batter into the pan.

→ Temperature control is key to great pancakes. Heavy skillets are ideal for their even heat distribution; they're far less prone to hot spots than thin pans. Keep your heat at or just below medium, use plenty of butter or oil, and don't be shy about shifting your pan around and off the flame to even out and control the heat as needed.

When Great Coffee Is the Only Option

The first time I ever went whitewater paddling was a four-day trip down a remote river in Quebec. The group I joined—friends of a friend—were nice enough, but not much for creature comforts. They ate rubbery, gray powdered eggs for breakfast and made the coffee "cowboy style"—stale, tin-can grounds dumped into a greasy pot with a slosh of barely boiled water. "It'll put hair on your chest!" one of them told me. The only thing worse than the taste of that coffee was the slurry of grounds you swallowed with every slug.

Ever since that trip, I've refused to compromise on coffee. I've tried pretty much everything through the years. I've carried mini-espresso machines and moka pots, percolators, French presses, packets of instant coffee, and over-the-top pour-over gear. I've ground my own beans in lightweight mills and experimented with nearly every type of pod. The only constant, year over year, is how rapidly the taste gap between at home and the wild has shrunk—to the point that, today, it barely exists.

Here's a rundown of the standout options, from simplest and lightest to the most gear-intensive and complex. Whether any of them will put hair on your chest, I couldn't say.

INSTANT

If your last taste of instant coffee was a sip of your grandmother's half-and-half-addled Nescafé, you're missing out. The best of them, made by craft coffee roasters, are as balanced and delicious as at many good shops. And if you're into Starbucks java, the company's VIA instant packets are widely available and thoroughly drinkable. Whichever brand you choose, a single serving weighs in at less than 10 grams.

POUR-OVER

Coffee grounds, a filter, and a stream of hot water; there aren't many simpler setups than this. Yet pour-over can also make a truly stellar cup. If you want to get super into technique, you'll find no end of instruction online. Otherwise, for a single serving, use 3 tablespoons of medium-fine grounds and 1½ cups of near-boiling water; pour the water over the grounds in three or four additions, pausing in between.

The pour-over gear options are nearly infinite, but a stack of paper filters and collapsible basket (I really like the inexpensive SOTO Helix) are all you need. You can also find superb craft-roasted, single-serve, pour-over packets that work a little like open-topped teabags; they perch, via a built-in holder, over the rim of your cup.

FRENCH PRESS AND AEROPRESS

Brew the coffee grounds and water in a chamber, then plunge them out through a filter. French presses give you more control over brew strength and flavor than other methods, but thanks to their fundamentally sad sack filtering mechanism, the coffee almost never comes out grit-free. AeroPresses push the coffee at pressure through a paper microfilter, so you'll never have to chew on grounds.

MOKA POT

Larger, fancier models of the classic Italian stovetop boilers are heavy and sometimes have compartments for frothing milk. For car and RV camping, they're nice. But for other camping styles, the smaller versions weigh in at around 1½ pounds and make the same thick, powerful, honeyed brew, one brain-defibrillating cup at a time.

ESPRESSO

A proper shot of well-balanced espresso in the wild seemed way too much to ask for until a few years back. But a series of handheld, pump-style machines has made superlative espresso shots a no-fuss (or at the very least, *medium-low*-fuss) reality. Some models use Nespresso pods while others rely on loose grounds and hand tampers. The simple, reasonably lightweight and (relatively) inexpensive machines from Wacaco—and particularly its Nanopresso model—have been among the best, although as with all things coffee, the market and technology are changing rapidly.

AND DON'T FORGET THE GRIND

For shorter and lightweight trips, pre-ground should please all but the most fanatical java heads. I usually ask the roaster to grind precisely to whatever brewing method I have planned. But still . . . freshly ground can be *really* nice, and working a camp mill's hand-crank feels strangely wax-on/wax-off meditative; at least to me. If that's your pace, Japanese craft coffee-gear company Hario makes a light and inexpensive model. And VSSL's fully adjustable, made-in-Canada metal-burr grinders are the high-end sports cars of manual coffee grinders; the one I've got does a better job than my fancy Italian countertop model at home.

My Go-To Granola
p. 177

Oui Je Parle French Toast

Serves: 4
Ingredient Weight: 23 ounces

This recipe is for the most gorgeously rich and custardy French toast you'll ever make or eat, with a kiss of orange and vanilla to put it way over the top. Better still, you mix the batter at home and freeze it in a little Nalgene bottle. Meaning you'll get The World's Best French Toast, Ever (if you don't mind my saying), in the wild. And its gratification comes pretty much instantly, like everything that's good and worth doing in life.

AT HOME

4 large eggs

⅔ cup heavy cream

¾ teaspoon granulated sugar

⅛ teaspoon kosher salt

3 drops vanilla extract

Zest of ½ orange

AT CAMP

Prepared batter (thawed) ❄

8 slices brioche, challah, or other soft white bread (thawed) ❄

2 tablespoons salted butter, plus more for serving (thawed) ❄

¼ cup pure maple syrup (thawed) ❄

KEEPS

The batter, 3 days, after thawing, kept cold

1. MIX, PACK, AND FREEZE

In a medium bowl, combine the eggs, cream, sugar, salt, vanilla, and orange zest and whisk until smooth.

Pour the batter into a leakproof container and freeze. (It will keep for 2 weeks, frozen.)

2. SOAK THE BREAD

Shake or stir the batter to mix. In a deep dish, pan, bowl, or large resealable bag, combine the bread slices and batter and let soak for 5 minutes, carefully turning the pieces as needed so they're uniformly wet.

3. COOK AND SERVE

In a medium or large pan over medium-low heat, melt ½ tablespoon of the butter (or more for larger pans), swirling the pan to coat.

Carefully transfer a few pieces of the battered bread to the hot pan. (The wet bread will be fragile.) Cook until the undersides are golden and lovely, about 3 minutes, then flip the pieces and cook until golden on the other side. The butter will burn a little; that's okay.

Wipe out the pan between batches as needed, add fresh butter, and repeat.

Serve the French toast, warm, with butter and the maple syrup.

Note

→ If you *must* substitute the heavy cream with milk (dramatic sigh), this will still make some very delicious French toast.

Chilaquiles

A classic Mexican Sunday brunch from Tijuana to Tapachula, chilaquiles are beloved around many a campsite too. They're brilliant whether simmered over a fire or prepared on a backpacking stove. You can make this version with one or both of the salsas, depending how much prep you feel like doing. The red salsa is a round-flavored, sweet tomato-and-chipotle number. The green is a more punchy-tasting tomatillo take.

And although this recipe calls for black beans and eggs, feel free to top these with almost any tasty protein: Seared, sizzling, well-seasoned strip steak; grilled pork; refried beans; shredded chicken; and Mexican chorizo are all superb.

AT HOME

Red Salsa

2 medium tomatoes

2 garlic cloves, skin-on

½ small yellow onion, skin-on

3 whole canned chipotle chilies in adobo sauce, plus 1 teaspoon of the sauce

1 cup packed coarsely chopped cilantro leaves and stems

¾ cup water

1½ teaspoons white vinegar

1 tablespoon vegetable oil

1 teaspoon kosher salt

1. MAKE ONE OR BOTH SALSAS

Preheat the oven to 450°F. If you're making both salsas, you can combine the vegetables on the same baking sheet.

For the red salsa: Place the tomatoes, garlic, and onion on a rimmed baking sheet. Roast until the vegetables are soft and browned in spots, 25 to 30 minutes. In a blender or food processor, combine the roasted tomatoes, garlic (skin still on), onion (skin still on), chipotles and 1 teaspoon sauce, cilantro, water, vinegar, vegetable oil, and salt. Blend or process until the salsa is smooth.

For the green salsa: Place the tomatillos, garlic, onion, and jalapeños on a rimmed baking sheet. Roast until the vegetables are soft and browned in spots, 25 to 30 minutes. In a blender or food processor, combine the tomatillos, garlic (skin still on), onion (skin still on), jalapeños, cilantro, water, vinegar, vegetable oil, honey, and salt. Blend or process until you have a coarse but not chunky salsa.

Pack the salsas in a leakproof container or resealable bag and refrigerate or freeze. (They will keep for 1 month, frozen.)

Green Salsa

5 canned whole tomatillos

1 garlic clove, skin-on

¼ small yellow onion, skin-on

3 jalapeño chilies, halved, seeded, and stems and white veins removed

1 cup packed coarsely chopped cilantro leaves and stems

½ cup water

1 teaspoon white vinegar

1 teaspoon vegetable oil

1 teaspoon honey

1 teaspoon kosher salt

AT CAMP

1 tablespoon salted butter (thawed) ❄

4 large eggs

1⅓ cups canned black beans, drained (thawed) ❄

Prepared salsa(s) (thawed) ❄

8 ounces unsalted tortilla chips

6 ounces crumbled feta or Cotija cheese (thawed) ❄

1 avocado, halved and pitted

1 cup sour cream

KEEPS

The salsas, beans, and cheese, 3 days, after thawing, kept cold; the eggs and sour cream, to their best-before date, kept cold (see Note, page 159)

2. COOK THE TOPPINGS

In a 10-inch or larger skillet over medium heat, melt the butter until the foaming subsides. Add the eggs and fry as you like them. Transfer to a plate and cover to keep warm.

In a small saucepan over medium-high heat, warm the beans to a simmer. Remove from the heat, and keep warm.

3. ASSEMBLE THE CHILAQUILES

In the skillet over medium-high heat, warm your choice of salsa to a simmer. Decrease the heat to medium-low and add the tortilla chips. If you like your chilaquiles fully saturated with sauce (or as some might put it, soggy), stir well. If you prefer crisp chips, don't.

Top the chilaquiles with the beans, the second salsa (if using), feta, and fried eggs and let simmer until heated through, about 2 minutes. Remove from the heat.

With a small spoon, scoop the avocado over the chilaquiles, along with dollops of the sour cream. Serve immediately.

Powdermilk Biscuits

Makes: 8 to 10 biscuits
Ingredient Weight: 21 ounces

I like to pull out this prepped-ahead, just-add-water mix near the end of a trip, when fresh-baked buttermilk biscuits are pretty much the last thing any camper expects. These biscuits are as easy to make as the ones from store-bought mix, but they're built on real lard (or shortening) and butter (with none of the additives). They're hot and golden and deliciously flaky—little buttery exclamation points straight out of the fire.

An inexpensive, lightweight biscuit cutter is the best way to get tall-rising biscuits, but you can also use a sharp knife if you'd prefer.

 Be sure to snap a photo of the Dutch oven instructions on page 225 before your trip!

SPECIAL EQUIPMENT

A 2½-inch biscuit cutter (optional)

AT HOME

2¼ cups all-purpose flour

¼ cup buttermilk powder

1 tablespoon baking powder

2 teaspoons granulated sugar

1 teaspoon kosher salt

¼ teaspoon baking soda

¼ cup lard or shortening, cut into chunks

¼ cup salted butter, cold, cut into chunks

1. MAKE THE QUICK BISCUIT MIX

In the bowl of a food processor, combine the flour, buttermilk powder, baking powder, sugar, salt, baking soda, lard, and butter and pulse to form a coarse mixture with pea-size butter and shortening chunks. If any bigger stubborn chunks remain, rub them into the flour with your fingers until they're pea-size or smaller.

Pack the biscuit mix into an airtight resealable bag or container, and refrigerate or freeze. (It will keep for 3 months, frozen.)

2. PREP A PARCHMENT SHEET

Trace the bottom of your Dutch oven onto a sheet of parchment paper. Cut out the outline and then pack it along with your Dutch oven.

3. START THE RIGHT FIRE

Get a baking fire going and preheat the Dutch oven lid as directed.

4. PREP YOUR WORK SURFACE

Dust a flexible plastic cutting board, large plate, or skillet with 1 tablespoon of the biscuit mix.

5. MIX AND KNEAD

Empty all but 2 tablespoons of the biscuit mix into a medium bowl, reserving the remaining portion for kneading and rolling. Pour the water evenly over the top of the biscuit mix and combine with a fork, spoon, or your fingers until a shaggy dough forms. (Don't worry if it doesn't all come together yet.)

Dust your hands with a bit of the reserved dry mix, then gently press the dough into a single mass inside the bowl. Knead five to ten times, just until the dough holds together. (If it absolutely refuses, you can add a teaspoon or so more water.) Transfer to the prepared rolling surface.

AT CAMP

Prepared quick biscuit mix (still frozen is fine, but not required) ❄

⅔ cup cold water

Butter and jam for serving (thawed) ❄

KEEPS

The dry mix, 1 week, unrefrigerated, or 2 weeks, kept cold

6. FORM THE BISCUITS

Make sure the parchment round is in the bottom of the Dutch oven.

Using a clean water bottle, roll the dough (or gently pat it out with your palms) into a ¾-inch-thick round or square, adding a sprinkle of dry mix as necessary to keep it from sticking.

If using a biscuit cutter, make eight to ten biscuits, reworking the scraps as necessary to form new biscuits. Flip the rounds upside down (it'll help them rise) and arrange in the prepared Dutch oven.

If using a knife, trim the outside edges (reserve the scraps), then cut the dough into nine even squares. Flip them upside down (it'll help them rise) and arrange in the prepared Dutch oven. Then form the scrap dough into a disc and tuck it into a gap to bake.

7. BAKE AND SERVE

Bake the biscuits for 6 to 12 minutes total, depending on your heat. Peek in on them after 6 minutes. If they still look like raw dough, instead of puffy steaming proto-biscuits, add coals under the Dutch oven and on top of the lid, and adjust the time accordingly.

When the biscuits are puffed and medium-golden, carefully remove the Dutch oven from the heat and transfer the biscuits to a plate to cool slightly. Serve the biscuits with butter and jam.

Excellent Overnight Oats

Serves: 7
Ingredient Weight: 3½ ounces per serving

This versatile oat, fruit, and nut mixture is my go-to for quick, delicious, on-the-go fill-ups. You can soak it overnight for no-cook and quick-cook versions, or simmer it from dry in 15 minutes. No matter how you do it, it's nutty, satisfying, and full of goodness, with a milky-sweet hit from the accompanying topper mix. The hemp hearts are worth seeking out for their mildly nutty flavor and healthy fats. For the mixed dried fruit, sour cherries and chopped pears, prunes, and apples are all excellent.

AT HOME

1⅓ cups steel-cut oats

⅔ cup mixed dried fruit, chopped if necessary

½ cup raw almonds, coarsely chopped

½ cup hemp hearts

¼ cup chia seeds

¼ teaspoon kosher salt

3 tablespoons brown sugar

3 tablespoons instant skim milk powder

AT CAMP (PER SERVING)

½ cup prepared oat mixture

1 to 1½ cups water, or ⅔ cup dairy of your choice (yogurt or milk)

Prepared topper mixture

KEEPS

1 month, unrefrigerated

1. MAKE THE OAT MIXTURE

In a resealable bag or container, combine the oats, dried fruit, almonds, hemp hearts, chia seeds, and salt.

2. MAKE THE TOPPER

In a second resealable bag or container, stir together the brown sugar and milk powder.

3. SOAK OR COOK, AND SERVE

Overnight Water Soak Method
For each serving, in a resealable bag or leakproof container, combine the oat mixture and 1 cup water and let soak overnight. In the morning, in a small saucepan over low heat, bring the soaked oats to a simmer.

Overnight Dairy Soak Method
For each serving, in a resealable bag or leakproof container, combine the oat mixture and yogurt and let soak overnight.

Forethought-Is-Not-My-Bag Method
For each serving, in a small saucepan over low heat, combine the oat mixture and 1½ cups water and let simmer, stirring occasionally, for 10 to 15 minutes, or until it's reached the oatmeal consistency of your dreams.

Serve the oats with the topper sprinkled over them.

Perfect Granola,
Every Time

For as long as I've been baking, I've been baking granola. Giant, freezer-filling, don't-need-to-make-breakfast-for-months-style batches, filled with top-quality bulk-store finds. Sometimes that granola has been absurdly tasty. Other times, the results haven't been quite . . . on point. There was the batch I'll never forget that I badly oversalted. And another that had about twenty times more flaxseed than it should. (It got awkward.)

Then a few years ago, food writer Anna Stockwell broke it all down in an online post, with a simple ratio even my embarrassingly non-math-grasping mind could understand. It goes like this.

3 parts rolled oats

+ 1 part raw, unsalted seeds

+ 1 part 50-50 liquid fat and liquid sweetener

+ 1 part raw, unsalted nuts

+ 1 part other (dried fruit, coconut, chocolate, etc.)

As for seasoning, I dialed that in: 1 teaspoon of kosher salt for every 6 cups of dry ingredients. I've never made a less-than-perfect batch since. But what's best about this formula is the versatility it provides. You can use pretty much any seed or nut. You can add wheat germ, hemp hearts, or buckwheat groats (file under "other"); chia seeds or sesame seeds; and whatever dried fruits will get you out of bed. (Dried peaches and pears can be seriously tasty, although I'm a dried-sour-cherry guy through and through.) Your choice of fats is nearly limitless (some granola-heads even use apple sauce). Your sweeteners can include maple syrup, honey, brown rice syrup, agave syrup, reduced apple cider, and even fruit molasses (a dash of the pomegranate variety for the win). All of it works, subject to your taste. All you need is to get the ratio right.

My Go-To Granola

Serves: 6 to 8
Ingredient Weight: 2 pounds

This recipe uses three types of nuts for roasty crunch and complex energy, plus a mix of seeds and dried sour cherries for their luxuriously tart-sweet chew. It's got maple syrup as the sweetener (so good!), plus a mix of coconut oil and olive oil—both healthy fats—to round it all out.

It's a pretty killer camping breakfast, and a deliciously dead-easy topper for fire-baked fruit.

Oats

3 cups rolled, old-fashioned oats

Seeds

½ cup hulled raw pepitas

¼ cup flaxseed meal

¼ cup raw sunflower seeds

Nuts

½ cup chopped walnuts

¼ cup chopped pecans

¼ cup chopped or slivered almonds

1 teaspoon kosher salt

Fat + Sweet

¼ cup melted coconut oil

¼ cup olive oil

½ cup pure maple syrup

Other

¾ cup tart dried cherries (see Note)

¼ cup golden raisins

KEEPS

1 month, unrefrigerated

1. MIX

Preheat the oven to 300°F.

In a large bowl, combine the oats, seeds, nuts, and salt, and mix well. Add the fat + sweet and stir well to coat.

2. BAKE AND PACK

Spread the mixture evenly on a large rimmed baking sheet. Bake the granola for 30 to 50 minutes, stirring once or twice, until golden, dry, and fragrant. Remove from the oven and stir in the dried fruit.

Let the granola cool, then pack in an airtight container or resealable bag and freeze whatever you don't plan to eat within 1 month. (It will keep for 3 months, frozen.)

Note

→ When you're using dried fruit, always add it *after* baking; time in the oven can quickly turn it hard and dry.

LUNCHES

Lunch is too often camping's forgotten meal.
Maybe because it happens when we're on the go, when we're hiking or paddling or packing up to move. Or because it can be hard for lunch to live up to breakfast's can't-miss-it importance and dinner's way of always stealing the show.
But wild lunch, done well, can also be the day's best eating. It's a fortifying pause, a tiny (or not so tiny) event, a chance to grab a breath and take in the view. And it's also, to its enduring credit, the mealtime without rules. It can be a ham-and-cheese sandwich eaten high above a set of switchbacks. It can be a buttery-lemony pan of freshly fried fish in a cove where you kayak-surfed to shore. It can be an instant, Alps-style fondue that's designed for backpacking stoves. Or maybe it's a tangle of dan dan noodles, studded with chili crisp and oven-dried pork, devoured with your friends on a lazy Sunday, when the only plan you won't let slide is to read that novel—at last—on a sun-warmed rock. Whatever your ideal, I've got you covered. Lunch is on.

Bikini Sandwiches

(aka The Most Sublime Grilled Cheese Toasties You'll Ever Taste)

Makes: 4 sandwiches
Ingredient Weight: 21 ounces

Bikini sandwiches, named for Barcelona's Sala Bikini music hall, are masterpieces of moderated gluttony. Made from cheese, ham, soft white bread, and salted butter, they're purposefully thin; decadent but inhalable. And they're always somehow tastier when prepped ahead—perfect. They travel from pack to plate in 10 minutes or less. These ones are inspired by my friends Tobey Nemeth and Michael Caballo, whose restaurant Edulis, in Toronto, is one of my favorite places on Earth.

AT HOME

6 ounces Emmenthal cheese, rind removed, very thinly sliced

4 ounces French ham (jambon de Paris), prosciutto cotto, or any unsmoked, thinly sliced ham

8 slices pain au lait, Pullman bread, or brioche

4 tablespoons salted butter, at room temperature

AT CAMP

Prepared sandwiches, unwrapped

KEEPS

3 days, kept cold

1. FILL THE SANDWICHES

Divide the cheese and ham among four slices of bread; a single layer of cheese, a single layer of ham (or if the meat's very thin, a double layer), and then another single layer of cheese. Cover with the remaining four bread slices.

2. BUTTER AND WRAP

Set each sandwich on a 12 by 14-inch sheet of wax paper or parchment paper.

Butter both sides of each sandwich, making sure the butter reaches all the way to the edges. (Butter gaps give bikini lovers the sads.)

Wrap the prepped sandwiches in the paper and secure with tape if you're not a wax-paper-wrap-master. Refrigerate.

3. TOAST AND SERVE

In a skillet set over low heat, toast each sandwich on both sides, pressing with the back of a spatula as they cook, until they turn perfectly golden and the interiors are melty, 6 to 10 minutes total.

Transfer the sandwiches to a plate and cut on the diagonal. Serve immediately.

Note

→ For a decadently high-low (and Barcelona baller-style) addition, shave or use a Microplane to grate most of a 1-ounce black truffle between the cheese and ham layers. Chop or grate the remaining truffle into 3 tablespoons of butter and use to butter the inside of the bread before topping the sandwiches. A fresh summer truffle should cost about the same as a good bottle of wine (anywhere between $20 and $50); it's just as intoxicating, but without the pack weight or hangover.

Fancy Not-Fancy Quesadillas

Serves: 4
Ingredient Weight: 42 ounces

My neighbor Alonso offered to make lunch when we took him and his family canoeing a few summers back. "I'm just going to make some quesadillas," he told us, as if it was nothing. Then he delivered the most ridiculously delicious lakeside meal we'd had all year.

Alonso's quesadillas combine pan-seared white cheese with blistered green beans and an inky, charry, burnt-pepper salsa. They're creamy and crunchy, milky and briny, wondrously dark-flavored and spicy (do not neglect to make the salsa!), and somehow wildly refreshing too. Better still, they're almost entirely prep-ahead, so they're ready in 15 minutes or less.

The chilies in this salsa pack a ton of spice. Kitchen gloves are always a good idea when handling them raw, and be sure to run your stove exhaust and open any windows through the charring step.

AT HOME

8 habanero or Scotch bonnet chilies, halved, and stems, ribs, and seeds discarded

2 garlic cloves, peeled

3 tablespoons extra-virgin olive oil

2 tablespoons white vinegar

1½ tablespoons water

Kosher salt

½ pound green beans, trimmed

1. CHAR THE VEG FOR THE SALSA

Set a dry, medium skillet over high heat. Add the habaneros and garlic, flattening the chilies against the pan with a spoon or spatula.

Roast the veg, turning every few minutes, until the chilies are mostly blackened, with just a few unburned spots, 10 to 15 minutes. (They should look almost like charcoal.)

2. PUREE AND PACK THE SALSA

Transfer the charred habaneros and garlic to a food processor, blender, or molcajete, along with the olive oil, vinegar, 1 tablespoon of the water, and ¼ teaspoon salt.

Process until reasonably smooth (a few small chunks are okay), adding the remaining ½ tablespoon water as needed to make the salsa thick but pourable.

Pack the salsa into a small, leakproof bottle and refrigerate.

3. PREP THE GREEN BEANS

Bring a medium saucepan of well-salted water to a boil over high heat. Add the green beans and let simmer until they're tender and mellow-tasting, 4 to 6 minutes.

Drain the beans, then rinse with cold water to cool. Drain again, and dry them in a salad spinner or on a clean kitchen towel.

Wrap the beans in paper towels before packing and then refrigerate.

CONTINUES →

AT CAMP

1 tablespoon extra-virgin olive oil (thawed) ❄

Prepared green beans

1 lemon, halved

Kosher salt

1 pound queso fresco (see Note)

Eight 6-inch corn tortillas

1 avocado, peeled, pitted, and sliced lengthwise into strips (optional)

Prepared salsa

KEEPS

The beans, 3 days, kept cold; the salsa, 3 weeks, kept cold; the cheese, to its best-before date, kept cold

4. BLISTER AND SEASON THE GREEN BEANS

In a large nonstick or well-seasoned skillet over medium-high heat, warm the olive oil.

Add the green beans to the skillet and sear, stirring only occasionally so they blister and color in the pan, 2 to 3 minutes.

Transfer the green beans to a small bowl or plate. Squeeze the juice of half the lemon over the beans, and season liberally with salt. Keep the beans warm while you prepare the quesadillas.

5. SEAR THE CHEESE; TOAST THE TORTILLAS

Drain the queso fresco of any liquid and pat it dry. Cut it into strips approximately ¼ inch thick for a total of sixteen strips.

Set the skillet over medium-high heat. Add two cheese strips and one tortilla alongside them. (If your pan is larger, feel free to make two quesadillas at a time.)

Sear the cheese on the first side until it's golden underneath, 30 to 45 seconds. Using a pancake (good) or fish (best) spatula, flip the cheese and then the tortilla. Sear for another 30 to 45 seconds—ideally, the queso fresco will be hot and melty but still reasonably intact, with a fragile, golden crust.

Place the cheese on the tortilla and top with a few green beans. Transfer to a plate.

Repeat with the remaining cheese and tortillas.

6. SERVE

Dress the quesadillas with the avocado, if desired, and serve immediately with the salsa on the side (it's spicy!).

Notes

→ Queso fresco, the pressed fresh cheese common around Latin America, Spain, and Portugal, comes in varying textures. You want firm for this recipe. Look for it in vacuum packs; it's typically firmer and longer lasting that way. You'll find it in many supermarket cheese sections as well as Latin-American grocers.

→ In case you're wondering why a salsa-covered, taco-like (taco-adjacent?), single-tortilla-based foodstuff is called a *quesadilla* and not a *taco*, it's because it's filled with cheese and griddled in a pan. Which officially makes it a quesadilla. Look it up!

→ The camping-leftovers-are-trouble rule does *not* apply to this salsa. It's pure magic on eggs, grilled meats, and vegetables.

Fire-Burst Tomato and Feta Dip

Serves: 4
Ingredient Weight: 2 pounds

This ridiculously elegant instant lunch is melty, creamy, and bursting with fire-roasted tomatoes, the briny punch of warm black olives, and the scent of fresh oregano. Think of it as Greek salad meets grill, and you're most of the way there.

AT HOME

⅔ pound mixed cherry tomatoes

⅔ cup pitted black olives

¼ small red onion, thinly sliced

1 tablespoon fresh oregano leaves, or 1 teaspoon dried

⅛ teaspoon granulated sugar

⅛ teaspoon kosher salt

2½ tablespoons extra-virgin olive oil

10 ounces solid (not crumbled) sheep's or goat's milk feta cheese (see Note)

Freshly ground black pepper

AT CAMP

1 garlic clove, smashed, peeled, and coarsely chopped (optional)

Prepared feta packet

8 ounces pita or sourdough bread

2 tablespoons extra-virgin olive oil (optional; thawed) ❄

KEEPS

3 days, kept cold

1. COMBINE

Cut a double layer of heavy-duty aluminum foil that measures 20 inches long, and lay it out horizontally in front of you.

In the middle of the foil, combine the tomatoes, olives, onion, oregano, sugar, salt, and olive oil, and toss to mix. Spread the vegetable mixture down the middle of the foil horizontally, stopping a few inches short at either end.

2. NESTLE, SEAL, AND PACK

Cut the feta into six to eight chunks, nestle them into the vegetables, and then season with several good grindings of pepper.

Gather the long edges of the foil together, folding them over each other two or three times to form a tight seal. Seal both ends of the packet in the same way.

Pack in a resealable bag or leakproof container and refrigerate.

3. ROAST THE PACKET

Add the garlic (if using) to the feta packet and reseal.

Place the packet on a grill over medium-hot coals. Roast until it's soft, sizzling, and delicious-smelling, 8 to 10 minutes.

Using tongs, transfer the packet to a serving plate, taking care not to split the foil.

4. GRILL THE PITA AND SERVE

Brush or drizzle the pita bread with the olive oil, if desired. Grill the bread over medium heat to warm through and gently toast, about 1 minute per side.

Carefully open the packet and serve with the grilled bread.

Note

→ Cow's milk feta also works in this recipe, but it won't be as soft or rich as sheep's and goat's milk versions.

Fast-Food
Shrimp Burgers

Serves: 4
Ingredient Weight: 2½ pounds

These sweet, juicy, seafood-studded shrimp burgers take 15 minutes to prep, freeze like a dream, and cook up almost instantly over a camp stove or a fire. Soft, sweet, brioche rolls or Wonder Bread–style hamburger buns are ideal here.

AT HOME

½ jalapeño chili, stemmed, seeded, and coarsely chopped

1-inch cube fresh ginger, peeled and coarsely chopped

1 small shallot, coarsely chopped

1½ pounds peeled shrimp (deveined, if preferred)

⅛ teaspoon kosher salt

AT CAMP

1 teaspoon vegetable oil (thawed) ❄

Prepared patties (thawed) ❄

4 soft hamburger buns (thawed) ❄

A few packets of single-serve, shelf-stable mayonnaise

Bread-and-butter pickles for serving

Shredded iceberg or butter lettuce or cabbage for serving (optional)

1 lime

KEEPS

The patties, 24 hours, after thawing, kept cold

1. CHOP IT ALL UP

In the bowl of a food processor, combine the jalapeño, ginger, and shallot and process until finely chopped.

Add half of the shrimp and the salt and process again to form a paste, using a spatula to scrape the sides of the bowl as needed.

Add the remaining shrimp to the processor and pulse to very coarsely chop and combine (there should be identifiable pieces of shrimp).

2. FORM THE PATTIES AND FREEZE

Line a baking sheet with wax paper or plastic wrap.

Using damp hands, form four patties and place on the prepared pan. Freeze until the patties are frozen solid, 2 or 3 hours.

Stack the patties, separating each one with wax paper or plastic wrap to prevent sticking. Wrap the stack tightly in plastic wrap. Place inside a wide-mouth Nalgene-type jar or repurposed plastic container, and freeze. (They'll keep up to 2 months, frozen.)

3. SEAR THE PATTIES

In a medium skillet over medium-high heat, warm the oil. Add the patties and sear until they're cooked through, nicely golden-crusted, and the shrimp has turned an appealing pink, 1 to 3 minutes per side.

4. TOAST, ASSEMBLE, AND SERVE

Toast the buns on a grill over medium heat. (Or toast the buns in the skillet over medium heat with a splash of oil or butter.)

Dress the buns with the mayo, assemble the burgers, and then garnish with pickles, lettuce (if using), and a squeeze of lime juice. Serve immediately.

Note
→ If you don't have a food processor, use a sharp knife, first to finely chop the vegetables and then to finely chop half of the shrimp into a paste. Coarsely chop the remaining shrimp, then combine all the ingredients and stir well.

Golden-Crisp Fish in Lemon and Caper Butter

Serves: 2 as a main, 4 as
        an appetizer
Ingredient Weight: 1½ pounds

You can always serve this as a main course, I guess. But, at least in my camp, it seems to become an impromptu appetizer—exactly the sort of unexpected snack that turns my friends all feral as they pluck up the sizzling, butter-sauced pieces with their hands. It's sweet, sour, and sunny-tasting from lemon juice; briny from capers; decadently velvety and nutty-flavored from browned butter; and crispy-crunchy, too, from its trip through a screaming-hot pan.

AT CAMP

1 pound fish fillets (see Note), skin-on or -off (thawed) ❄

¼ cup Because-Somebody's-Gonna-Catch-a-Fish Mix (facing page)

1 teaspoon olive oil or vegetable oil (thawed) ❄

2 tablespoons salted butter (thawed) ❄

1 lemon, halved

2 tablespoons capers, drained and rinsed

KEEPS

Up to 2 days, kept cold

1. COAT THE FILLETS

Pat the fillets dry. If the skin's been left on, using a sharp knife, score it in a shallow crosshatch pattern.

Pour the fish mix onto a wide plate or into a bag, and dredge each fillet to coat completely, shaking off any excess. Discard any used fish mix.

2. SEAR THE FISH

Set a medium or large skillet over medium-high heat and add the olive oil and 1 tablespoon of the butter.

Once the butter is melted and sizzling, add the fish (skin-side down) and sear until it's golden brown, 2 to 4 minutes. Flip each fillet and sear until the flesh is cooked through and the second side is nicely colored, another few minutes. (The thicker the fillets, the more time they'll take.)

3. WHIP UP THE SAUCE

Squeeze the lemon's juice over the fish. Transfer the fish pieces to a serving plate, and keep warm. Remove the skillet from the fire or burner, letting the residual heat thicken and sweeten the butter and citrus sauce forming in the pan.

Off the heat, add the capers and remaining 1 tablespoon butter to the skillet, mixing the sauce with a fork or whisk while it bubbles. (If the pan cools too quickly, you can briefly stick it over the heat again as needed.)

4. SERVE

Pour the sauce over and around the fish, or simply return the fish to the pan. Serve immediately.

Note

→ You can make this dish with almost any fish species, although mild, white-fleshed varieties such as bass, pike, and walleye are extra-delicious, as are trout, salmon, and saltwater flatfish. And although this recipe calls for 1 pound of fillets, adjust it up or down as needed. (Two pounds would be ideal as a lunch for four people.)

Because Somebody's-Gonna-Catch-a-Fish Mix

Makes: Enough to coat about 4 pounds of fish

Ingredient Weight: 5½ ounces

This make-ahead flour mix comes as close as you'll get to a guarantee of perfectly seasoned fish. It has just the right amount of salt to bring out any fish's natural sweetness without overwhelming it, and enough sneaky background heat from black pepper and cayenne to bring the flesh alive. Simply dredge your seafood in the mix, shake off the excess, fry or sear in oil or butter, and serve.

AT HOME

1 cup all-purpose flour

1½ tablespoons kosher salt

2 teaspoons cayenne pepper

1 teaspoon freshly ground
    black pepper

KEEPS

Up to 6 months, unrefrigerated

1. MIX

In a large resealable bag, combine the flour, salt, cayenne, and black pepper. Seal and shake until combined.

Such a Nice Salad

Serves: 4
Ingredient Weight: 5 pounds

If there's a fresher, healthier, more delicious salad-slash-meal than a Niçoise, I've never found it. It's boiled new potatoes and tender green beans bathed in an herby-mustardy-anchovy dressing you could eat with a spoon. It's briny black olives and halved hard-boiled eggs, plus a jar—or a few pack-friendly pouches—of oil-packed tuna to top it all off. And sure, it's also elegant and French, but in a hearty-lunch-in-the-Pyrenees kind of way.

For the eggs and vegetables, review "Of Course You Can Bring Eggs!" on page 15.

AT HOME

4 large eggs

4 teaspoons kosher salt

1 pound green beans or yellow wax beans, trimmed

1 pound mini, fingerling, or small new potatoes, scrubbed and halved

1 tablespoon white vinegar

3 anchovy fillets (salt-packed and rinsed, or oil-packed)

1 garlic clove, finely chopped

2 tablespoons cider vinegar or white wine vinegar

2 tablespoons Dijon mustard

1 small shallot, thinly sliced

½ cup best-quality extra-virgin olive oil

1. PREP THE EGGS

Fill a medium saucepan with 2 quarts of cold water. Fill a medium bowl with water and ice cubes to make an ice bath.

Add the eggs to the saucepan, cover, set over high heat, and bring to a simmer. Turn off the heat and let the eggs cook in the hot water for 10 minutes.

Using a slotted spoon, scoop the eggs from the pan and transfer to the ice bath. Let sit until chilled, about 10 minutes.

2. PREP THE BEANS

Turn the heat under the saucepan to high and return the water to a boil.

Add 1 tablespoon of the salt and the green beans to the water and cook until the beans become just tender and mellow-tasting, 4 to 6 minutes.

Turn off the heat, and using tongs or a spider strainer, transfer the beans to a colander or fine-mesh sieve. Run cold water over them to cool, then let them dry on a clean kitchen towel.

3. PREP THE POTATOES

Return the pot to the high heat and let it come back to a boil.

Add the potatoes and white vinegar. Decrease the heat to medium and cook at a low boil until the potatoes are tender, 12 to 24 minutes.

Drain the potatoes, then let cool on a clean kitchen towel.

4. PREP THE DRESSING

Finely chop the anchovies, then add the chopped garlic and remaining 1 teaspoon salt and, using the side of your knife, drag-smoosh them into a paste.

In a medium bowl, combine the anchovy paste with the cider vinegar, mustard, and shallot. Slowly drizzle in the olive oil while whisking to emulsify. Stir in the parsley and herbs, then season with pepper.

1 cup flat-leaf parsley leaves, coarsely chopped

2 tablespoons mixed fresh tender herbs (thyme, tarragon, and chervil are all great), coarsely chopped

Freshly ground black pepper

AT CAMP

Prepared eggs

1 pound mixed cherry tomatoes

Prepared beans and potatoes

¾ cup Niçoise or Kalamata olives

10 ounces oil-packed chunk light tuna, drained and broken into hunks (see Note)

Prepared dressing (thawed) ❅

KEEPS

The prepped vegetables, olives, eggs, and thawed dressing, 3 days, kept cold

5. PACK

Transfer the eggs to a resealable container (or egg carton) and refrigerate.

Roll the vegetables loosely in paper towels, then pack in a resealable bag or container and refrigerate.

Pack the dressing in a resealable container and refrigerate or freeze. (It will keep for 1 month, frozen.)

6. MIX, DRESS, AND SERVE

Peel and halve the eggs, then halve the tomatoes.

In a serving bowl or on a platter, combine the eggs and tomatoes with the beans, potatoes, olives, and tuna.

Shake the dressing well to re-emulsify, then dress the salad (toss it or simply drizzle on top, your call). Serve immediately.

Notes

→ Italian tuna packed in jars with olive oil is beautiful stuff, worth seeking out. Regular canned or vacuum-pouched chunk tuna will also be delicious though.

→ You can also assemble and dress the salads individually.

Pack-Bottom Sesame Slaw

Makes: 4 servings
Ingredient Weight: 4 ounces
  (dressing only); 1 pound
  (with slaw ingredients)

I blame/credit this one entirely on my (excellent, lovely) wife, Carol. She likes her crunchy vegetables, cruciferous ones in particular. On Day 4 or 5 of any wilderness trip, she'll reach deep into one of our food bags and extract a fat wedge of green cabbage. This bright, nutty, deliciously silky dressing is the perfect slaw topper. And a lot like Carol's sneaky cabbage stashes, it can last seemingly forever at the bottom of a pack.

AT HOME

1 tablespoon white sesame seeds

1 tablespoon white miso paste

2 tablespoons toasted sesame oil

1 tablespoon granulated sugar

2½ tablespoons unseasoned
  rice vinegar

1 teaspoon water

AT CAMP

¾ pound raw slaw-appropriate
  vegetables and fruit (fresh or dried),
  nuts, and seeds (see Note)
Prepared dressing (thawed) ❄

KEEPS

The dressing, 2 weeks, unrefrigerated, or 1 month, kept cold

1. TOAST THE SEEDS

In a dry, small skillet over medium heat, toast the sesame seeds, stirring frequently, until they're golden and fragrant, 3 to 5 minutes.

2. MIX AND PACK THE DRESSING

In a medium bowl, whisk the miso paste, sesame oil, sugar, vinegar, and water to form a smooth, silky emulsion. Stir in the sesame seeds.

Pack the dressing in a small leakproof container and refrigerate or freeze. (It will keep for 2 months, frozen.)

3. CUT THE SLAW AND DRESS

Shred, chop, or thinly slice the vegetables and fruits as desired. Transfer to a serving bowl and combine with any nuts or seeds.

Shake the dressing to re-emulsify, then dress the salad before serving.

Note
→ Green and red cabbage, carrots, green apples, shredded raw beets, sesame seeds, pepitas, and dried fruit are all ideal here. (A bag of store-bought slaw mix also wouldn't be a horrible thing.)

Fire-Grilled Corn,
p.136

The Crunch and Freshness Everybody Craves after a Few Days Out

No matter what the menu or type of trip, most campers can hold out in the wild for only so long before thoughts of juicy, crunchy freshness start to fill their waking dreams. So, get ahead of those cravings with a few delicious gimmes. They're grouped by how long you can expect them to last in a pack in moderate temperatures.

You can generally add a couple of extra days for anything kept cold, while hot weather will shorten their longevity. (For more on how to wrap and pack perishable foods, see "Of Course You Can Bring Eggs!" on page 15.)

SHORT-LASTING (UP TO 3 DAYS)

→ Cilantro, parsley, tender herbs

→ Firm, fresh plums and sweet cherries

→ Japanese and Korean supermarket pickles (daikon, burdock root, mustard greens, and pickled ginger are always standouts)

MEDIUM-LASTING (3 TO 5 DAYS)

→ Cherry tomatoes

→ Green onions

→ Lebanese cucumbers

→ Lemons

→ Rosemary, sage, and thyme

→ Unripe avocado

LONG-LASTING (5 DAYS PLUS)

→ Hardy apple varieties, especially Gala, Fuji, and Granny Smith

→ Whole beets (terrific raw and thinly sliced)

→ Unwashed green and red cabbage, either whole (most stable) or quartered

→ Large, unpeeled, uncut carrots

→ Whole, uncut ginger root

→ Kimchi and sauerkraut (they'll get funkier as they age)

→ Dehydrated lemon and lime slices (see "Turn Your Oven into a No-Frills Dehydrator," page 202)

→ Preserved lemon peel (packed in a bit of its brine)

→ Limes

→ Onions, shallots, and garlic

Street-Festival Sausage and Peppers

Serves: 4
Ingredient Weight: 4 pounds

The only thing better than eating sausage and red peppers at an Italian street festival is eating them in the wild, especially when the sausages are grilled over a fire. They get smoky and blistery and bursting with juiciness; the red peppers and onions nearly melt in their own natural sweetness. Add a crusty roll to soak it all up and that's amore.

AT HOME

4 large red, orange, or yellow bell peppers, stems, cores, ribs, and seeds discarded, sliced into ¼- to ½-inch strips

2 medium yellow onions, thinly sliced

4 sprigs thyme

2 sprigs oregano

¼ cup extra-virgin olive oil

AT CAMP

4 large Italian sausages (sweet fennel or spicy are ideal; thawed) ❄

Prepared pepper-onion mixture

2 garlic cloves, coarsely chopped

¾ teaspoon kosher salt

Freshly ground black pepper

4 white-bread rolls

Mustard for dressing (optional)

KEEPS

The vegetable mix, 5 days, kept cold; the sausages, up to 3 days, after thawing, kept cold

1. PACK THE PEPPER-ONION MIXTURE

In a resealable bag or leakproof container, combine the bell peppers, onions, thyme, oregano, and olive oil and refrigerate.

2. START THE SAUSAGES

Grill the sausages over medium-hot coals until they're cooked through and nicely browned, 8 to 12 minutes. (Alternatively, in a medium skillet over medium heat, warm 1 teaspoon of the oil from the bottom of the pepper-onion mixture. Add the sausages and pan-roast until they're cooked through and nicely browned, 10 to 15 minutes.)

3. COOK THE PEPPERS AND ONIONS

Meanwhile, set a medium or large skillet over medium-low heat. Dump in the pepper-onion mixture and chopped garlic, season with the salt, and slowly cook, tossing and stirring frequently, until the vegetables are very soft and caramelized in spots and the pan juices have cooked off, 20 to 30 minutes. (If the sausages finish cooking before the vegetables are done, set them aside for a breather.)

4. ASSEMBLE AND SERVE

Add the sausages to the pan to combine the flavors. Season with plenty of black pepper, then mound everything to one side of the pan.

Split the rolls, then, one by one, press them into the empty space in the pan and toast. (Adding an extra splash of olive oil wouldn't be wrong.)

Add a sausage to each roll, pile with the caramelized vegetables, and dress with mustard, if desired. Serve immediately.

Instant Caramelized Shallot-Cheese Fondue

Serves: 4
Ingredient Weight: 2½ pounds

This is exactly the dish you pull from your pack at 7,500 feet as a storm blows past. It's also exactly the dish you pull from your pack while car camping on a crisp fall day when everybody's got rosy cheeks and ridiculous smiles and they're high on that whole outdoor life thing. Wherever you make it, this one-pot lunch is drop-dead easy and crazy delicious, and it will make you a bona fide backcountry (or KOA-country) star.

AT HOME

1 tablespoon salted butter

3 small shallots, thinly sliced

¼ teaspoon kosher salt

12 ounces Gruyère cheese,
    rind removed

1 tablespoon cornstarch

Scant ⅛ teaspoon freshly grated nutmeg

AT CAMP

1 cup dry white wine (thawed) ❄

Prepared cheese and shallots
    (thawed) ❄

1 crusty baguette

A few hardy, crunchy dippables such
    as endive leaves or apple slices

KEEPS

3 days, unrefrigerated, or up to 1 week, kept cold

1. CARAMELIZE THE SHALLOTS

In a small skillet over low heat, melt the butter. Add the shallots and salt and let them caramelize slowly and gently, stirring occasionally, until they're tender, sweet-tasting, and an appealing hazelnut brown, 15 to 25 minutes.

Let the shallots cool, then wrap tightly in a small piece of parchment paper or wax paper.

2. PREP THE CHEESE

Meanwhile, over a small bowl, grate the Gruyère on the coarse side of a box grater. Add the cornstarch and nutmeg and toss to combine thoroughly.

Pack the cheese mixture into a resealable bag or airtight container, stick the packet of caramelized shallots inside the bag (on top of the cheese), seal the bag, and refrigerate or freeze. (The cheese mix and shallots will keep for 1 month, frozen.)

3. MELT, BURBLE, AND SERVE

In a small saucepan over medium heat, bring the wine to a simmer. Add the cheese mixture and shallots. Decrease the heat to low and stir to melt the cheese.

Once the cheese has melted and the fondue is bubbling gently, decrease the heat to its lowest setting. Your goal is warm, very gently bubbling cheese. If your stove's lowest setting has the cheese bubbling furiously, feel free to shuttle the pan on and off the burner.

Serve the fondue with sliced or torn bread and crunchy dippables, as well as forks if there are known double-dippers in your midst.

Turn Your Oven into a No-Frills Dehydrator

When pack weight matters or coolers aren't an option, simple home dehydrating is the easiest way to keep on eating well in the wild. It's how you get ground meats, tofu, mushrooms, and jerky after days on an alpine trek, or the taste of citrus when you've been island-hopping in a kayak for weeks on end. Although purpose-built dehydrators are the most efficient option, it's easy to use your home oven as a dehydrator too. (These tips and recipes apply regardless of which you use.)

THE BASICS

THINK THIN
The thinner the food is, the more quickly it will dehydrate. Keep fruit, veg, and jerky slices to ¼ inch or thinner. When browning meat before dehydrating, be sure to break it into the smallest chunks possible.

LEAN IS BEST
For meats you plan to keep for more than a few weeks, always buy lean (good) or extra-lean (best), and blot away fat with paper towels. Animal fats go rancid fast. For the same reason, avoid adding unstable fats before dehydrating; a bit of sesame, olive, or vegetable oil is okay if you must (it can help with pre-dehydration searing) but the trade-off is less longevity. If you plan to consume your dehydrated goods within a few weeks, though, a bit of fat can pay enormous rewards in flavor.

SEASON FIRST
It's easiest to get flavor into meats and tofu when they're still fresh, so do your seasoning before you dehydrate.

CRUMB YOUR MEAT, FREEZE YOUR TOFU
The cook behind backpackingchef.com, Glenn McAllister, developed a trick to dry ground proteins so they come out tender at camp, instead of rubbery-crunchy. Add ½ cup of breadcrumbs or ground rolled oats per 1 pound of ground beef, pork, or lamb. For tofu, freeze it in its package, then thaw it and press out the water before dehydrating.

LOW TEMPS = BETTER DRYING
Home-oven heat dials typically start between 150° and 200°F, and many toaster ovens go even lower. Although you'll get good results anywhere in that range, most fruits, vegetables, and tofu dehydrate best at 135°F, mushrooms at 125°F, and ground meats at 145°F. Use those temps if you've got them.

AIRFLOW IS EVERYTHING
If your oven has a convection setting, use it. The fan helps push out moisture. If not, crack your oven door open an inch. (A wooden spoon handle's good for this.) And wherever possible, lay sliced or larger pieces of food on wire racks (the cooling racks used in baking are great) to dry, so they don't stay wet on one side.

DRY GROUND MEAT, GOOD; RAW GROUND MEAT, NOT SO MUCH
Always cook ground beef, pork, and lamb all the way through (it should be at 160°F) before dehydrating; poultry requires a minimum cooked temperature of 165°F.

SEAL WELL AND FREEZE

Let dehydrated meat and tofu cool thoroughly, seal in airtight bags or containers, and freeze until your trip. It will generally keep for 6 months, frozen. Unrefrigerated, 2 weeks to 1 month is my (conservative) rule of thumb. Dehydrated fruit and mushrooms can be more susceptible to moisture. I leave mine in an unsealed bag for the first week after dehydrating, and check it frequently for any signs of moisture or spoilage.

DEHYDRATED GROUND BEEF, PORK, OR LAMB

Add ½ cup of unseasoned breadcrumbs or ground rolled oats per 1 pound of extra-lean meat. Knead with your fingertips to incorporate, then let stand for 5 minutes. Season if desired.

In a large, dry, nonstick skillet over high heat, brown the meat, chopping and stirring aggressively with a flat wooden spoon or spatula to break up the chunks. Blot the meat well with paper towels, then transfer to a parchment paper–lined pan in a single layer. Dehydrate at your oven's lowest temperature (145° to 170°F is ideal, although up to 200°F will work), stirring occasionally, for 5 to 6 hours, or until the pieces are hard and their insides are dry. Blot again to remove remaining fat.

DEHYDRATED MUSHROOMS

Clean the mushrooms with a damp paper towel, then trim their stems. Slice into ¼-inch pieces. Arrange on a cooling rack and dehydrate at your oven's lowest setting (125°F is ideal) until the pieces snap when bent, 4 to 5 hours.

DEHYDRATED TOFU

Freeze firm or extra-firm tofu in its package, then let thaw. Press the tofu well to drain any water, then slice, chop, matchstick, crumble, or cube it into pieces no more than ¼ inch thick. Marinate it if you'd like, or sear it with sauce or seasonings.

In a nonstick skillet over high heat, warm 1 teaspoon of sesame oil or other cooking oil, then add the tofu and brown well. Transfer the pieces to a drying rack and dehydrate at your oven's lowest temperature (135°F is ideal, up to 200°F is okay) for 6 hours, or until they're dry inside and snap when you try to bend them.

DEHYDRATED CITRUS

Wash lemons, oranges, limes, or grapefruit well, then slice into ¼-inch rounds. Dehydrate at your oven's lowest temperature (135°F is ideal) until they're dry but still pliable, about 6 hours. (They'll become more brittle as they cool.)

HOW TO REHYDRATE

Cover ground proteins with boiling liquid and let stand for 10 to 15 minutes, or simmer in liquid or sauce until tender. For fruit and mushrooms, cover with warm or boiling water and let stand for 15 to 30 minutes. You can also drop dried, sliced citrus directly into drinks.

Dan Dan Noodles of Backcountry Dreams

Serves: 2 to 4
Ingredient Weight: 30 ounces

It's hard to think of a more in-your-face-delicious backpacking meal than this fiery, sweet, sour, and savory noodle dish. It's got crisp fried pork and steaming wheat noodles, and is topped with toasted peanuts and Sichuan peppercorns. And it's bathed in a chili crisp–based sauce that's dark and brooding and puckery-tangy from black rice vinegar. Thanks to simple home-oven dehydrating, the high-protein ground pork—exactly what your body will crave after miles on the trail—can last for weeks on end in a pack.

For the dehydrated pork, review "Turn Your Oven into a No-Frills Dehydrator" on page 202.

AT HOME

8 ounces lean ground pork

5½ teaspoons soy sauce

¼ cup plain breadcrumbs

One 7-ounce jar Sichuan chili oil or spicy chili crisp (see Note)

1 garlic clove, finely chopped

1½ tablespoons Chinkiang vinegar

1½ tablespoons granulated sugar

½ cup unsalted peanuts

½ to 1 teaspoon Sichuan peppercorns

1. COOK AND OVEN-DEHYDRATE THE PORK

In a small bowl, combine the pork, 1 teaspoon of the soy sauce, and breadcrumbs and knead the mixture with your fingertips until fully incorporated. Let stand for 5 minutes. Meanwhile, line a large plate with paper towels.

In a dry medium, nonstick skillet over high heat, add the pork mixture and sear, breaking it up with a spatula or spoon, to thoroughly brown and crisp the meat, 8 to 12 minutes.

Transfer the pork to the prepared plate to drain, blotting well to remove excess fat, then dehydrate and pack as directed.

2. PREP THE SAUCE

In a small bowl, combine ⅓ cup of the chili oil (liquid only; you may need to top with vegetable oil if there's not enough in the jar), 3 tablespoons of the chili oil solids, garlic, vinegar, sugar, and remaining 4½ teaspoons soy sauce and stir well.

Transfer the sauce to a leakproof container and refrigerate or freeze. (It will keep for 2 months, frozen.)

3. PREP THE SICHUAN PEANUT TOPPING

In a dry small skillet over medium heat, toast the peanuts and peppercorns until the nuts begin to sizzle gently and color and the peppercorns are nicely fragrant, 2 to 4 minutes. Let cool.

Using a rolling pin or mortar and pestle, smash the nuts and peppercorns into a coarse mixture. Transfer to a small container or resealable bag.

CONTINUES →

AT CAMP

Prepared dehydrated pork mixture (thawed) ❄

¾ cup water, plus more for cooking the noodles

⅓ cup Sichuan ya cai (see Note)

12 ounces thin Chinese wheat noodles or udon

Prepared sauce (thawed) ❄

Prepared peanut topping

4 green onions, thinly sliced (optional)

KEEPS

The prepared sauce and ya cai, 5 days, unrefrigerated, or 2 weeks, kept cold; the green onions, 5 days, kept cold

4. REHYDRATE THE PORK

In a medium skillet over medium heat, combine the dehydrated pork and water and bring to a simmer. Cook off most of the water, stirring occasionally, 5 to 8 minutes.

Before the pork is completely dry, add the ya cai to the pan and stir to warm through. Remove from the heat and set aside.

5. COOK THE NOODLES

Boil the noodles according to the package instructions. When they're nearly done, scoop ¼ cup of the noodle water from the pot and reserve.

6. ASSEMBLE AND SERVE

Meanwhile, divide the prepared sauce among your bowls.

When the noodles are done, drain and divide among the bowls over the pools of sauce.

Top the noodles with a splash of the reserved cooking water to loosen them. Add the pork and the peanut topping, then garnish with the green onions, if using. Toss to coat, and serve.

Notes

→ Chili oil types and brands can taste wildly different, from brightly fruity and floral to dark and brooding. Although they'll all work well in this recipe, keep your eyes out for small-batch versions. Whichever one you pick, be sure it's not just oil but a combination of oil and chili solids. And if you're still at a loss, go for the Laoganma brand Spicy Chili Crisp in the red jar. (You'll know it by the famous founder's face on the package.) It makes a ridiculously delicious dan dan base.

→ Ya cai, the savory mustard-stem preserve, is painstakingly air-dried, double-fermented, and then boiled in sugar and spices. It adds unmistakable flavor and depth. The ya cai made by Sichuan Yibin Suimi Yacai Co. is the gold standard for dan dan noodles. You can find it in some Chinese grocers or online. Ask for Yibin Suimi Yacai, or look for the characters 碎米芽菜 on the package. You can also substitute zha cai (pickled mustard tuber), which can be easier to find.

→ Vegan option: At camp, in place of the pork, cover **twenty-four dehydrated shiitake mushroom caps** with boiling water for 20 minutes to rehydrate. Drain, gently squeeze the water from the mushrooms, and then slice thinly. Sear in a hot pan with **2 teaspoons neutral oil** and **2 teaspoons soy sauce** until the mushrooms are nicely colored. Add the ya cai and ½ cup water, stirring to break up the greens. Cook off the water (the mixture should be moist, but not wet), and then serve.

Super Ramen!

(How to Make Instant Noodles Delicious)

When I first started backpacking, I lived off packaged ramen. Whatever those instant noodles lacked in flavor and nutritional value, they more than made up for in wham-bam, thank-you-Mr.-Noodle-Man convenience. My packaged ramen fix was filling, cheap, lightweight, and easy. And then one afternoon in Montana, on an otherwise spectacular subalpine hike, my love—or maybe let's call it purely carnal infatuation—turned into an all-out loathing.

What rekindled the affair, a solid decade later, was an egg, a few sliced green onions, a bit of roasted seaweed, and a tablespoon of miso paste. Those no-frills noodles became richly bodied, nutritious, and deeply satisfying—with a brightness and crunch I haven't stopped craving since.

The trick to any instant-ramen remake is to throw out a good half of the seasoning that comes with it. Then add at least one delicious thing from four key categories.

STIR IN A FLAVORING

→ Chinese chili oil or spicy chili crisp

→ Chinkiang or rice vinegar

→ Dasida (Korean instant beef stock)

→ Kimchi

→ Lime juice

→ Red or white miso

→ Sambal oelek (Indonesian vinegared chili paste)

→ Shiitake or porcini mushroom powder

→ Soy sauce or tamari

→ Ssamjang

SLIP IN A PROTEIN

→ BBQ Chinese duck

→ Fresh fish

→ Fresh or dehydrated tofu

→ Poached egg

→ Pork loin and belly, or beef (available at Chinese and Korean supermarkets), frozen and then sliced thinly

→ Roast, BBQ, or braised pork

→ Tinned mackerel

ADD STURDY GREENS

→ Collards, kale, or green cabbage, very thinly sliced

→ Napa cabbage kimchi (also a flavoring)

→ Sliced green onions (also a garnish)

→ Whole spinach

FINISH WITH A GARNISH

→ Dried seaweed (seasoned snacking seaweed and seaweed salad mixes are my go-to's)

→ Fresh, frozen, or dehydrated corn kernels

→ Katsuobushi (shaved, dried skipjack tuna; also a flavoring)

→ Pickled daikon

→ Seasoned, preserved burdock root

→ Store-bought fried shallots

→ Toasted white or black sesame seeds

CONTINUES →

A Few Super Options

HOT POT(ISH)

1 packet instant noodles

+ half of its seasoning powder

+ 1 tablespoon ssamjang

+ pre-sliced frozen beef

+ thinly sliced green cabbage

+ toasted sesame seeds

MISO PORK

1 packet instant noodles

+ half of its seasoning powder

+ 1 tablespoon miso paste

+ sliced BBQ pork

+ 1 egg poached in the pot as the noodles cook

+ 1 sliced green onion

+ sliced pickled daikon

SPICY SEAFOOD

1 packet instant noodles

+ half of its seasoning powder

+ 1 tablespoon sambal oelek

+ ½ tin mackerel packed in oil

+ 2 sliced green onions

+ fried shallots

VEGAN

1 packet instant noodles

+ half of its seasoning powder

+ a dollop of spicy chili crisp

+ a few pieces of quick-seared tofu (fresh or dehydrated)

+ a handful of spinach leaves wilted in the pot as the noodles cook

+ 1 sliced green onion

+ corn kernels

Vegan Super Option

A LITTLE SOMETHING FOR DESSERT

We lived on a hobby farm when I was growing up.

It was 2½ acres, nice size, with a forest in the front and a sloping pasture out back. In the summer, my dad would pitch our old canvas tent on the lawn behind the house. It smelled of mildew and neglect, but we loved it anyway.

We'd camp out there, my sister and me and our favorite cousins, in cheap and no doubt highly flammable sleeping bags that were printed on their insides with cowboy scenes. At night, after dinner, we'd run down to the pasture, where my dad always seemed to have a brush pile to burn. As we all stood waiting, he'd start one—whooooomp!—with a jerry can of gas.

As the brush pile burned, all us kids sharpened long, green alder branches for what was to come. Roasted marshmallows are the world's most perfect dessert. They're light and sweet and pure entertainment. What other dessert can a preteen wave on a stick after lighting it on fire—a corn syrup, gelatin, and tetrasodium pyrophosphate comet whooshing against the sky? My sister and cousins toasted them slowly. I'd incinerate them layer by layer, peeling and eating and howling with joy. But you don't need a recipe for that, I guess.

Then how about a moist and subtly tangy chocolate chunk cake? Or roasted end-of-summer stone fruit dolloped with a cloud of wild-whipped cream? There's drunken Spanish fruit and lemony Dutch babies, killer fire-baked sticky buns, and even a couple of boozy after-dinner drinks. And the hot chocolate recipe is pretty much begging for roasted marshmallows on top.

Roasted Stone Fruit

with Wild-Whipped Cream

Serves: 4 to 6
Ingredient Weight: 2 pounds

Warm, ripe, peak-season fruit flecked with vanilla sugar and caramelized on a glowing fire. The whipped cream—shaken up in a wide-mouth water bottle—is almost too much delicious. Almost, but also not at all. For the stone fruit, peaches, plums, nectarines, apricots, and cherries are all ideal.

SPECIAL EQUIPMENT

Heavy-duty aluminum foil,
18 inches wide

AT HOME

¼ cup granulated sugar

Zest of ½ lemon

½ vanilla bean

AT CAMP

1½ pounds fresh, ripe stone fruit

Prepared vanilla sugar

1 cup cold whipping cream (thawed) ❄

KEEPS

The vanilla sugar, 6 months,
unrefrigerated

1. PREP AND PACK THE VANILLA SUGAR

In a small bowl, combine the sugar and lemon zest.

Using a sharp knife, slit open the vanilla pod, then scrape its sticky black pulp—the seeds—into the lemon sugar. Reserve the pod. Rub the mixture with your fingers to break up the pulp and distribute it evenly.

Transfer the vanilla sugar and reserved pod to an airtight container or resealable bag. (The pod will add flavor when the fruit roasts.)

2. CHOP, SEASON, AND WRAP THE FRUIT

Remove the pits from the fruit, then chop the fruit into bite-size pieces.

Cut a double layer of heavy-duty aluminum foil that measures 22 inches long. Transfer the fruit onto the foil and arrange lengthwise down the middle of the foil, stopping 2 inches shy of either end.

Sprinkle the fruit with the sugar, add the vanilla pod, and toss to coat. Gather together the long edges of the foil, folding them over each other two to three times to form a tight seal. Seal both ends of each packet in the same way—you want to avoid any leaking.

3. ROAST THE FRUIT

Set the foil packet on a grill placed over medium-hot coals, or directly in the ashes beside them. Roast the fruit, turning the packet occasionally, until it feels very tender through the foil and smells incredible, 15 to 25 minutes.

Cut a hole through the top of the packet and continue roasting until the juices have reduced and thickened and the pieces of fruit are beginning to color in spots, about 5 minutes more.

4. WHIP THE CREAM AND SERVE

Meanwhile, pour the whipping cream into a clean, 32-ounce, wide-mouth water bottle and seal. Shake vigorously until the cream forms soft peaks (or your arms give up), 4 to 8 minutes.

Spoon the roasted fruit and its juices into bowls or mugs, then top with dollops of the whipped cream. Serve immediately.

Gingery
Baked Apples

Serves: 4
Ingredient Weight: 2 pounds

These are buttery, walnut-y, and tartly sweet, stuffed with ginger and orchard-fruit jam, then roasted to near collapsing in an after-dinner fire. Simple, yes, *and* highly effective. Far worse things have been said about dessert.

Quince paste, the Iberian preserve also known as *membrillo*, is ideal for the stuffing, with its refreshing (and out-of-the-ordinary!) fruit-blossom acidity, although plum or apricot jam make fine substitutes.

Fully prepped ahead, these apples work equally well in a Dutch oven or simply wrapped in packets of heavy-duty aluminum foil. And they double very nicely as an indulgent breakfast too.

 Be sure to snap a photo of the Dutch oven instructions on page 225 before your trip!

AT HOME

⅓ cup coarsely chopped walnuts

¼ cup golden raisins

2 tablespoons brown sugar

1 tablespoon membrillo, or plum or apricot jam

One ½ by ½-inch piece crystallized ginger

4 firm, medium apples (preferably Fuji or Gala)

½ lemon

3 tablespoons salted butter, cut into 4 pieces

1. MAKE THE FILLING

In a small bowl, combine the walnuts, raisins, and brown sugar.

Slice and then coarsely chop the membrillo and ginger and add to the bowl. (If you're using jam, simply dollop it in.) Stir well to combine, being sure to un-clump any sticking bits.

2. CORE THE APPLES

Wash the apples, then use a melon baller or a sturdy measuring teaspoon to excavate the cores from the stems down, making sure not to break through the apples' bottoms.

Squeeze the juice from the lemon half into the apples' holes, then rub the lemon's cut side on any exposed apple flesh.

3. STUFF

Stuff the apples with the filling (it may not all fit), then press a butter piece into the top of each hole, like a cap. Using a sharp knife, score each apple's skin around its waist.

4. PACK

If you plan to roast the apples in foil, cut a double layer of heavy-duty foil that measures 20 inches long. Arrange the fruit snugly on the foil. Gather together the long edges of the foil, folding them over each other two to three times to form a tight seal. Seal both ends of each packet in the same way—you want to avoid any leaking. If you'll be using a Dutch oven, wrap each apple in foil or plastic to prevent the filling from falling out. Refrigerate.

AT CAMP

Prepared apples

¼ cup water, brandy, or cider

1 cup cold heavy cream
(optional; thawed) ❄

Up to 3 days, kept cold

5. BAKE THE APPLES AND SERVE

Foil Method

Clear out a patch in your fire's coals so the packets won't be sitting directly on the embers. Open the packet, add the water, and re-seal. Mound the coals around but *not on* the packets, then roast for 10 to 30 minutes, rotating the packets frequently and adjusting the coals as necessary, until the apples are very soft through the foil.

Dutch-Oven Method

Unwrap the apples and place them in the Dutch oven, right-side up. Add the water, cover with the lid, and bake until the apples are extremely soft, 20 to 30 minutes.

Serve the apples straight up, or with a drizzle of cream or instant custard, if desired.

Fire-Baked Pecan Sticky Buns

Makes: 6 buns
Ingredient Weight: 42 ounces

When I was growing up, there was a German bakery near my house that was famous for its cinnamon rolls. They were basically stuffed to overflowing with chopped roasted nuts and gooey cinnamon–brown sugar. When you pulled off a piece, those rolls released a cloud of steam that made non-cinnamon-roll thoughts impossible. Those rolls were my introduction to what's now called "mindful eating." I'm grateful I got to bypass all the study and asceticism and fast-forward instead to the nut-sugar nirvana state.

These sticky buns are as close as I've tasted to the cinnamon rolls of my youth. You bake them, fully prepped from your cooler, in an after-dinner fire. As you pull the Dutch oven from the fire and lift the pot's lid, quietly intone the words *Fire-Baked Pecan Sticky Buns*. That phrase should reach your friends just as the cinnamon steam envelops them. Nirvana is so much closer than most people think.

SPECIAL EQUIPMENT

An 8- or 9-inch cake pan that fits inside your Dutch oven with the lid on, or an 8- or 9-inch foil Dutch-oven liner

---

 Be sure to snap a photo of the Dutch oven instructions on page 225 before your trip!

1. MAKE THE DOUGH

In a small saucepan over low heat, warm the milk to just slightly above body temperature. (Alternatively, microwave on full power to lukewarm, but not hot.)

In the bowl of a stand mixer fitted with the dough hook, combine the warm milk, flour, yeast, granulated sugar, melted butter, egg, and salt.

Run the mixer at low speed until a soft, sticky dough forms. Increase the speed to medium-low and knead until the dough is smooth and springs back when poked, 8 to 10 minutes. (Alternatively, mix the dough with a spatula, then knead by hand for roughly 12 minutes.)

2. LET IT RISE

Form the dough into a ball, place in a large bowl, cover with plastic wrap, and set in a warm spot to rise until it doubles in size, 60 to 90 minutes.

3. PREP THE PAN

Trace the bottom of the cake pan or liner onto a piece of parchment paper. Cut out the outline and then use it to line the inside bottom of the pan or liner.

4. MAKE THE SAUCE

In a small saucepan over medium heat, combine the butter, Demerara sugar, maple syrup, and pecans. Cook, stirring, until the sugar crystals have melted, about 2 minutes.

Pour into the prepared cake pan and transfer to a freezer to chill.

5. MAKE THE FILLING

In a medium bowl, combine the pecans, Demerara sugar, cinnamon, and salt, and mix well.

6. ROLL AND FILL

Once the dough has risen, dust a clean surface and a rolling pin with flour. Transfer the dough to the surface, dust it with flour, and

Dough

½ cup whole or 2% milk

2 cups plus 2 tablespoons all-purpose flour, plus more for dusting

1¾ teaspoons instant yeast

2 tablespoons plus 2 teaspoons granulated sugar

3 tablespoons salted butter, melted and cooled

1 large egg, at room temperature

½ teaspoon kosher salt

Sticky Sauce

3 tablespoons salted butter

¼ cup packed Demerara sugar

2 tablespoons pure maple syrup

⅓ cup raw pecans, coarsely chopped

Filling

⅔ cup raw pecans, finely chopped

⅔ cup packed Demerara sugar

1½ tablespoons ground cinnamon

¼ teaspoon kosher salt

3 tablespoons salted butter, very soft

AT CAMP

Prepared buns (thawed) ❄

KEEPS

The raw buns, after thawing, kept cold, should be baked within 24 hours

then roll it into a roughly 10 by 10-inch square.

Using a spatula, spread the butter on the dough so it covers all but a ¼-inch strip at one edge. Sprinkle the filling evenly over the butter, then rub and press it into the dough.

Roll the dough toward the unbuttered edge, gently pulling any slack to form a tight cylinder. Press the seam to seal the dough securely.

7. CUT, PACK, AND FREEZE

Using a sharp knife, cut the dough cylinder into six equal buns. Arrange the buns on top of the sauce in the prepared, chilled pan.

Press a sheet of wax paper into the pan so it touches the tops of the rolls. Use a sheet of aluminum foil (or a very large, resealable freezer bag) to seal the pan well, then freeze. (The buns will keep for up to 3 weeks, frozen.)

8. WARM AND RISE

Remove the wax paper from the thawed buns and allow them to warm to air temperature and rise. The buns should swell to nearly touching in roughly 30 minutes, if it's hot out, or 2 hours, in colder temperatures. If the air temperature is cooler than 68°F, warm gently in the covered Dutch oven, beside the fire.

9. START THE RIGHT FIRE AND BAKE

Bake the buns following the instructions on page 224. After 15 minutes, take a quick peek. The buns should be fully risen and starting to firm up. If they are baking too slowly (they still look raw) or too fast (they're nearly done), add or remove coals and adjust the baking time accordingly.

The buns should take between 30 and 40 minutes total. When they are firm and deep golden, carefully remove the Dutch oven from the fire, then remove the cake pan from the Dutch oven.

10. SERVE

Run a clean knife around the inside of the cake pan to release the buns' edges. Place a clean plate on top of the cake pan and then carefully invert, so the buns and sticky sauce fall onto the plate and the sauce runs into the buns. Serve warm.

Drunken Spanish Fruit

Serves: 4
Ingredient Weight: 14½ ounces

This classic Spanish dessert, called *compota de frutas secas*, is nothing more than mixed dried fruit simmered until it's plump and tender, then steeped with sweet sherry and pine nuts.

It's brilliant anywhere, but especially for backpacking. The lightweight ingredients can last weeks in a pack, especially if you oven-dehydrate the citrus. If you'd rather use fresh citrus, a couple slices each of lemon and orange will do. For the mixed dried fruit, prunes, apricots, pears, peaches, raisins, figs, and cherries are all ideal.

AT HOME

1 orange

1 lemon

2 cups mixed dried fruit

AT CAMP

Prepared dried fruit and citrus mix, or a few slices of fresh citrus

1½ to 2 cups water

3 tablespoons pine nuts

¼ cup sweet sherry (such as Pedro Ximénez) or other sweet dessert wine (thawed) ❄

1 cup heavy cream (optional; thawed) ❄

KEEPS

2 weeks, unrefrigerated, or 1 month, kept cold

1. DEHYDRATE THE CITRUS (OPTIONAL)

Preheat the oven to 150°F.

Cut away the pithy tops and bottoms of the orange and lemon, then cut the fruit into very thin rounds, about ⅛ inch thick; a mandoline slicer is ideal to use here.

Dehydrate as directed in "Turn Your Oven into a No-Frills Dehydrator," page 202.

2. MIX THE FRUIT AND PACK

In an airtight container or resealable bag, combine a few rounds each of the dehydrated orange and lemon with the dried fruit.

3. BURBLE IN WATER

In a small saucepan over medium-high heat, combine the fruit mix with enough of the water to cover. (If a few bigger pieces stick out a bit, that's okay.) Bring to a simmer, then decrease the heat to low. Let burble gently until the fruit is soft, plump, and fragrant and only a few tablespoons of the liquid remain, 15 to 20 minutes.

4. ADD THE SHERRY, STEEP, AND SERVE

Add the pine nuts and sherry to the saucepan. Stir to combine, then remove from the heat, cover, and let steep for 10 minutes. Serve the fruit warm or cold, straight up, or drizzled with the cream.

Backwoods Birthday Cake for an Excitable Child

Serves: 8 to 10
Ingredient Weight: 1½ pounds
  (plus optional icing and
  decorations)

This chocolate cake is a blockbuster bit of camping magic. It's rich and moist and uncommonly indulgent, with hunks of melted milk chocolate. It's smooth and serious, but also refreshingly bright-tasting (hello, powdered buttermilk). Whether you choose to decorate it—I like the works: sprinkles, glitter, dragées, nonpareils, and a whole tub of store-bought frosting—or eat it straight, you can't walk past without taking just one more slice.

SPECIAL EQUIPMENT

An 8-inch cake pan that fits in your Dutch oven with the lid on, or an 8-inch aluminum-foil Dutch oven liner (optional but highly recommended; see Note)

 Be sure to snap a photo of the Dutch oven instructions on page 225 before your trip!

AT HOME

1½ cups all-purpose flour

½ cup natural (non-Dutch-processed) cocoa powder

½ cup granulated sugar

½ cup packed Demerara sugar or dark brown sugar

2 tablespoons buttermilk powder

1 teaspoon baking soda

½ teaspoon kosher salt

½ vanilla bean

1. MAKE THE DRY MIX

In a medium bowl, combine the flour, cocoa powder, granulated sugar, Demerara sugar, buttermilk powder, baking soda, and salt.

Using a knife, slit the vanilla bean pod and scrape the sticky black seeds into the bowl. Discard the pod.

Whisk the dry mix (a few small brown sugar lumps aren't the end of the world) and transfer to a large resealable bag or reusable container.

2. PREP A PARCHMENT SHEET

Trace the bottom of your cake pan or liner onto a piece of parchment paper. Cut out the outline and then pack it along with the pan or liner.

3. START THE RIGHT FIRE

Get a baking fire going and preheat the Dutch oven lid as directed.

4. PREPARE THE PAN

Generously grease the bottom and sides of your cake pan or liner with some of the 1 tablespoon butter. Place the prepared parchment round on the buttered bottom of the pan, then butter the parchment as well. Set the pan inside the Dutch oven.

5. MIX AND POUR THE BATTER

You can mix the cake batter in your resealable bag if it's large enough, or transfer the dry mix to a medium bowl. Add the water and ⅓ cup melted butter and stir well to form a smooth batter; then stir in the chocolate chips.

Pour the batter into the prepared pan and gently shake the pan to level it out.

CONTINUES →

1 tablespoon salted butter
(thawed) ❄ , plus ⅓ cup,
melted and cooled

Prepared dry mix

1½ cups water

½ cup milk chocolate chips or chunks
(thawed) ❄

1 container store-bought icing,
plus decorations (optional)

The dry mix, 1 month, unrefrigerated

6. BAKE!

Bake the cake according to "Everything You Need to Know about Dutch Ovens" on page 224. After 15 minutes, take a quick peek. The edges should be more cake than batter; the baking should be nearly halfway done. If the cake is baking too slowly (it's mostly batter) or too fast (it's nearly done), add or remove coals from above and below and adjust the baking time accordingly.

The cake should take between 30 and 40 minutes. When the top looks fully baked and the sides are beginning to pull away from the pan, poke with a small knife, toothpick, or wooden skewer to test for doneness; it should come out clean.

Carefully remove the Dutch oven from the fire and then remove the cake pan, if using. Let cool to the touch.

7. DECORATE (OR NOT) AND SERVE

Run a sharp knife around the pan's inside edge and place a large plate on top of the pan. Carefully invert the pan onto the plate; the cake should slide out. Remove the parchment paper, then use another plate to invert again so the cake is right-side up.

If decorating (as garishly as possible), let the cake cool completely before doing so. (Icing and hot cakes don't get along.) Cut into wedges and serve.

Note

→ A cake pan or an aluminum-foil liner helps to insulate the batter from scorching heat, so your Dutch-oven cakes aren't nearly as likely to burn. Although you can also line your Dutch oven with parchment paper and pour the batter directly into it (I call that technique "the dump and pray"), I don't recommend it.

Everything You Need to Know about Dutch Ovens

Friends of ours gave us a cast-aluminum camping Dutch oven a few years ago. I remember thinking at the time it was pretty much the dumbest camp-cooking implement I'd ever seen. Dutch ovens are heavy—nearly 4 pounds in the case of my newest piece of gear. And besides all that, who wants to bake when they're in the wild?

It took just one paddling trip and a batch of buttery, golden, fire-baked biscuits (see page 172) before I put those reservations to rest. In that first season alone, I baked simple breads, cakes, and bubbling fruit crisps—the sort of fresh-made luxuries I'd never imagined eating in the wild. And that pot wasn't just an oven, either. I used its upturned lid as a griddle for flatbreads, and the 4-quart base for slow-simmered beans and fire-top stews.

If you paddle (without too many long portages), car or RV camp, or ski or backpack in groups where you can split up the gear, a lightweight Dutch oven can dramatically improve your camp cooking. Here's what you need to know.

WHAT TYPE TO BUY

Camping Dutch ovens aren't the same as the Dutch oven you may have in your kitchen. They have high-rimmed lids so you can pile them with embers for top-down heat. They don't come in nice colors either—or with any finish, generally—because they're meant to go straight on a fire. And the best ones for baking are relatively shallow. That's so their top-down heat can get to your food.

CAST IRON OR ALUMINUM?

If you're not a self-propelled camper, Lodge Camp and Camp Chef make quality cast-iron ones. I'm a far bigger fan of the anodized aluminum Dutch ovens from GSI Outdoors. They weigh about a third as much, are far easier to care for (to wit: they don't rust), and are every bit as durable too. And although anodized aluminum doesn't have cast iron's heat retention, I find that's a benefit for live-fire cooking; it's far more responsive when you need to increase or decrease the heat.

SIZE

I like a 10-inch shallow pot for its weight-to-usefulness ratio. It fits an 8- or 9-inch cake pan or up to a 10-inch aluminum-foil liner nicely. (*Cook It Wild*'s Dutch-oven recipes are designed for this size.) If you routinely camp with more than six people, consider a 12- or 14-inch one.

GETTING THE RIGHT TEMPERATURE

Some camp-baking fans use charcoal briquettes; they're more predictable than live-fire embers. But if you're not into hauling bags of briquettes into the wilderness, you probably need a different method, yes? With a few basic pointers, you can nail (fairly) consistent heat either way.

Block the wind, retain the heat: A fire pit that's ringed with high rocks or metal will reflect heat back to your Dutch oven and block BTU-stealing wind.

Build the right fire: The best fire for baking has a good bed of glowing embers, plus a few small logs burning off to one side to replenish the supply.

Clear a baking space: Once your fire's going, sweep or shovel out a space in the fire pit that's big enough to accommodate your oven with a few inches all around. That space should be bare ground or ash, without any residual coals. In case of wind or colder temperatures, build that space directly up against the fire ring for added radiant heat.

Mind the gap: If your Dutch oven has built-in legs, you're good to go. Otherwise, place a Dutch-oven stand or three strategically placed rocks in the center of your cleared space to raise the pot 2 to 3 inches above the ground. Be sure to level the stand if you don't love lopsided baked goods.

Heat the lid: Stick your Dutch oven's lid in the fire to give it a head start. I usually do this about 10 minutes before I'm ready to bake. (Just remember to use a fire glove or lifter when you pull it out!)

Dial in the heat: Use tongs or a shovel to place hot coals evenly inside the baking area. For most baking, you want the coals to cover no more than one-fourth of the ground under the pot. Place the filled Dutch oven over the coals and carefully replace its preheated lid. Now transfer hot coals onto the oven's lid; you want more on top than are under the pot, covering around one-third of the lid's area.

TO BAKE

Carefully rotate the Dutch oven a quarter-turn every 5 to 8 minutes of baking. This will help even out any hot spots. Rotate its lid a quarter-turn the opposite way.

TO USE BRIQUETTES

Here's a simple formula that'll work for 8-, 10-, or 12-inch ovens. For a 350°F Dutch oven, multiply the oven's diameter in inches by two, then add one briquette. So, for a 10-inch oven, you'll need twenty-one hot briquettes. Put one-third of the lighted briquettes under the Dutch oven, and the remaining two-thirds on its lid.

For higher or lower baking temperatures, add (or subtract) two lit briquettes to the formula for each change of 25°F.

Lemon-Sugar Dutch Baby

Serves: 2 to 4
Ingredient Weight: 18½ ounces

This easy Dutch-oven dessert is part pancake, part sweet soufflé. As it bakes in the fire, it puffs up golden and steamy and gently custardy, and its edges crisp and sweeten into an ultralight crust. Eat it hot from the pan with fresh lemon and a blizzard of sugar.

 Be sure to snap a photo of the Dutch oven instructions on page 225 before your trip!

AT HOME

½ cup all-purpose flour

2 teaspoons granulated sugar

¼ teaspoon kosher salt

½ cup whole milk

3 large eggs

Zest of ½ lemon

AT CAMP

Prepared dry and wet mixes (thawed) ❄

3 tablespoons salted butter (thawed) ❄

2 tablespoons granulated sugar

1 lemon

KEEPS

The wet mix, after thawing, kept cold, should be used within 2 days

1. MAKE THE DRY MIX

In a resealable bag or airtight container, combine the flour, sugar, and salt.

2. MAKE THE WET MIX

In a medium bowl, whisk together the milk, eggs, and lemon zest.

Pack into a leakproof container and freeze.

3. START THE FIRE

Get a baking fire going and preheat the Dutch oven lid as directed.

4. MIX THE BATTER

Meanwhile, in a medium bowl, whisk together the dry and wet mixes until combined and the batter is smooth.

5. BAKE

Place the empty Dutch oven over the coals.

Wearing fire gloves and working quickly, add the butter to the pan and swirl to coat, using a spatula as necessary to spread it up the Dutch oven's sides. Carefully pour in the prepared batter, then cover with the hot lid and place hot coals on top.

Bake, rotating the Dutch oven every 5 minutes, until the Dutch baby is puffed and golden, 8 to 12 minutes. (When you peek, do it quickly; Dutch babies deflate fast.)

6. SERVE

Remove the Dutch oven from the fire, then sprinkle the granulated sugar over the Dutch baby, which will deflate as soon as it cools.

Zest the lemon onto the Dutch baby and then slice (I usually do this right in the pot). Cut the zested lemon into wedges, squeeze its juice over the Dutch baby. Serve immediately.

Note

→ The batter should be at or close to air temperature at the start of baking; cold batter doesn't inflate as well.

Buttered-Rum Coffee Cake

Serves: 8
Ingredient Weight: 32 ounces

This sweet and boozy five-minute dessert combines store-bought pound cake with dark rum, espresso, and sweetened condensed milk. Slip the cake through sizzling brown butter, soak it with booze, drizzle on the make-ahead sauce, and then hit it with lime.

AT HOME

1½ to 2 ounces espresso or
  very strong coffee

¾ cup sweetened condensed milk

AT CAMP

Prepared coffee sauce (thawed) ❄

5 tablespoons salted butter, cut into
  pieces (thawed) ❄

12 ounces pound cake,
  cut into 8 slices

¼ cup dark rum (thawed) ❄

1 lime

KEEPS

The sauce, 5 days, after thawing, kept cold; the pound cake, check the best-before date

1. PREP THE COFFEE SAUCE

In a small bowl, combine the coffee and condensed milk and stir well to mix.

Pack the sauce into a leakproof container and freeze. (It will keep for 1 month, frozen.)

2. WARM THE SAUCE AND BROWN THE BUTTER

In a small saucepan over low heat, warm the sauce, stirring well to combine. (It will have separated in the freezer.) Cover and keep warm.

In a large skillet over medium heat, melt the butter. Cook, swirling the pan or stirring frequently until the milk solids at the bottom of the skillet turn light hazelnut, and the butter smells nutty. Be careful not to burn the butter—it can happen fast!

3. SIZZLE THE CAKE AND SERVE

Decrease the heat to medium-low and slip the pound cake slices into the skillet. Sizzle them in the butter until they're lightly golden and warm, and then flip, about 20 seconds per side. Immediately transfer the cake slices to serving plates or a platter, and soak them with the rum. Drizzle with the warm coffee sauce.

Using a Microplane grater, zest the lime over top. Halve the lime and squeeze the juice around the cake slices. Serve immediately.

The Toddy You Didn't Know You Needed

Makes: 6 drinks
Ingredient Weight: 17 ounces

This mellow, complex campfire sipper from star Toronto pastry chef and cocktail whiz Farzam Fallah gets gentle, chocolatey bitterness from Italy's Amaro Averna, sweetness from honey and bourbon, and a lift from orange fruit and peel. It's exactly the right drink for cool, clear nights under the stars.

AT HOME

2 tablespoons clover or wildflower honey

2 tablespoons boiling water

5 ounces bourbon

5 ounces Amaro Averna (Amaro Montenegro or Nonino are also fine)

AT CAMP

3 cups boiling water

Prepared toddy mixture (see Note; thawed) ❄

1 small orange, sliced, or 6 dehydrated orange rounds (see Note)

KEEPS

The toddy mixture, up to 2 weeks, unrefrigerated

1. MAKE THE TODDY BASE

In a small heatproof bowl, combine the honey and boiling water. Stir to make a syrup.

In a flask or leakproof container, combine 1¾ ounces of the syrup, the bourbon, and Amaro. Refrigerate or freeze. (Save the remaining ¼ ounce syrup for another use.)

2. MIX AND SERVE

Pour a splash of the boiling water into six mugs to warm them for a couple minutes, or warm them by the side of the fire. Dump out the water (or recycle it back into your kettle for a quick reheat).

Evenly divide the toddy mixture among the mugs. Top with 2¼ cups boiling water and garnish each toddy with an orange slice. Serve immediately.

Notes

→ Hot toddies, people love. Lukewarm toddies, not so much. Be sure your mugs are warmed, your water's boiling, and the base mix and orange are at air temperature or warmer before you mix the drinks.

→ For how to make dehydrated orange rounds, see "Turn Your Oven into a No-Frills Dehydrator," page 202).

Make-Your-Own Boozy Hot Chocolate Mini-Bottle Bar

Serves: 4
Ingredient Weight: 18 ounces
  (with all the fixings);
  9 ounces (with just the
  chocolate mix)

Super-chocolatey homemade cocoa. A stash of airline-style mini bottles. Late-night campfire party stokers don't really come better than this.

AT HOME

1 cup instant powdered skim milk

2 tablespoons cocoa powder (preferably natural; not Dutch-processed)

2 tablespoons Demerara sugar or dark brown sugar

3 ounces best-quality dark chocolate (preferably 70 percent), coarsely chopped

AT CAMP

Prepared cocoa mix

2 cups water

Toasted marshmallows for topping (optional)

Your gnarliest collection of mini-bottle booze

KEEPS

The dry mix, 2 months, unrefrigerated

1. MAKE THE DRY MIX

In a blender or the bowl of a food processor, combine the milk powder (start with this to avoid clumping!), cocoa powder, Demerara sugar, and chopped chocolate and whiz into a coarse powder. (If it clogs at all, no big deal. Just loosen the mixture and resume.)

Pack into a resealable bag.

2. MAKE A SMOOTH BASE PASTE

In a small saucepan over low heat, combine the cocoa mix and ½ cup of the water. Whisk thoroughly, then warm gently until the paste is smooth and glossy, 1 to 2 minutes. This step will eliminate any lumps.

3. SIMMER AND SERVE

Increase the heat to medium and whisk in the remaining 1½ cups water. Bring to a simmer and whisk thoroughly until it's perfectly smooth, around 1 minute.

Pour the hot chocolate into mugs and top with toasted marshmallows, if desired. Serve immediately, accompanied by miniature booze bottles to add as you see fit.

Notes

→ The natural cocoa powder and dark chocolate give this beverage a richly chocolate-forward flavor with plenty of acidic/fruity/bitter notes depending on the type of bar you use; for a more mellow cup, use Dutch-processed cocoa and milk chocolate.

→ The hot chocolate will thicken as it sits; add hot water as required.

Acknowledgments

I will forever be grateful for the snowy night several years back, sitting around a fire with Sasha Seymour, Yotam Tintpulver, Nancy Tong, Laas Turnbull, and my wife, Carol Toller, when I foolishly blurted, "You guys should come camping with us!" That original crew of accomplished indoorspeople—and the annual trips we started taking—inspired more of the deliciousness in this book's pages than I could ever count. To Sasha Seymour, in particular, chef, food stylist, recipe whisperer, and dear friend, I will always, always owe you huge.

Kirsten White and Darcy Killeen helped shape a couple novice paddlers into seasoned trippers over the years and provided immeasurable help with this book. You can borrow my tarp any time.

David Sax, Andrew Rowat, bestie Boyd Erman, Emma Reddington, Mika Bareket, design hero Rose Pereira, Krysta Look, and David Childerhose lent early advice, work, and support. Agent Judy Linden's brilliant edits and insights have been beyond invaluable throughout. David Zilber, Gail Simmons, Eden Grinshpan, Amanda Cohen, and Matty Matheson provided key backing when the book was in proposal stage, for which I'll always be grateful.

Claire Tansey took countless calls, texts, and not-at-all-angsty emails as I was writing—on recipes, food, and life questions large and small, and always in the world's greatest phone voice. Elspeth Copeland was also a constant go-to, with incisive, real-world recipe and ingredient advice. Recipe tester/ pastry god Camilla Wynne made it all work, and provided occasional talk therapy by text, while actual therapist Sean "the Master" Meggeson kept my head on straightish most of the time. (I never doubted I could do this, haha.)

Leandro Baldassarre, Neil Dowson, Mike McKenzie, Tobey Nemeth and Michael Caballo, Cynthia Leung and David Castellan, Mitchell Bates, Christopher Terpstra, Peter Sanagan, Afrim Pristine, Todd Youngson, Farzam Fallah, Alonso Gómez, Iago and Nacho Gómez Heredia, and Michael Raviele helped with cooking, food and recipe questions, and inspiration, while Jodi Greenwood, Jehan Paul-Chowdhury, Ted Bytalan (hi, Unc!), and Michael and Thomas Summers furnished key help on gear and camping.

Rob Mifsud, Chip Pitfield, Michelle Savoy, Di Hilton, Blanca Heredia, Ula Ubani, Kevin and Laurel Service, and Phil Lee gave important recipe feedback,

and Toby Lennox promoted the book to random backpackers in the Jasper wilderness with carnival-barker aplomb.

Photo team Maya Visnyei, Sasha Seymour, Eshun Mott, Rachel Cicoria, Lisa Daly, and Sumi Siddiqa, I will be forever grateful for your vision, skill, and grace in making high-pressure, off-grid, water-access-only, pit-toilet-serviced shoots feel (almost, sorta) effortless—and for rolling with that tornado warning. Model-friends Phil Lee, Katy Chan, Sheila Flaherty, Dylan and Grace Hopman, Brenda Ha, Mya Sandhu, Blanca Heredia, Mateo Gómez Heredia, and Laurel Service provided photogenic hands, faces, and plenty of good humor. Nikole Herriott, thanks for the prop loaners (and I'm still really sorry I broke your beautiful dish!).

On Georgian Bay, *merci* to Richard Auger, Michel Quintas, and the staff at Gilly's Snug Harbour Restaurant and Marine, plus Ian Merringer for local intel, and excellent Dino and Lia Dell'Orletta (and gang), who let our crew into your campsite.

Illustrator Claire McCracken understood the book and its vision pretty much immediately and delivered gorgeous work to bring it to life.

At Clarkson Potter and Penguin Canada, dream team Jennifer Sit, Francis Lam, and Andrea Magyar got behind the book early with smarts and enthusiasm. To them, designer Robert Diaz, senior art director Stephanie Huntwork, copyeditor Mi Ae Lipe, proofreader Linda Bouchard, production manager Kelli Tokos, and the entire editorial crew, a million thank-yous.

And last but so not least, Carol and Cormac, who've been on this hike from the start, with endless patience, love, first edits, support, and bug spray, let's go camping just for fun really soon, okay?

Index

Published in the United States by
Clarkson Potter/Publishers, an
imprint of Random House, a division
of Penguin Random House LLC,
New York
RandomHouseBooks.com
ClarksonPotter.com

CLARKSON POTTER is a trademark
and POTTER with colophon is a
registered trademark of Penguin
Random House LLC.

Library of Congress Cataloging-in-
Publication Data is on file with
the publisher.

ISBN 9780593-57847-6
eISBN 978-0-593-57849-0

Printed in China

Photographer: Maya Visnyei
Photography Assistants:
Rachel Cicoria and Sumi Siddiqa
Food Stylists: Sasha Seymour and
Eshun Mott
Editor: Jennifer Sit
Editorial Assistant: Bianca Cruz
Designer: Robert Diaz
Production Manager: Kelli Tokos
Compositor: Merri Ann Morrell and
Nick Patton

Copy Editor: Mi Ae Lipe
Proofreader: Linda Bouchard
Indexer: Ken DellaPenta
Marketer: Andrea Portanova
Publicist: Jana Branson

Book and cover design by
Robert Diaz
Cover photographs by
Maya Visnyei

10 9 8 7 6 5 4 3 2 1

First Edition

CHRIS NUTTALL-SMITH is a celebrated journalist,
food writer, and critic, as well as a *Top Chef Canada*
resident judge. Chris has also served as food editor,
chief restaurant critic, and dining columnist at *Toronto
Life* and national food critic for *The Globe and Mail*.
His writing about food and other subjects has appeared
in *The Wall Street Journal*, *Lucky Peach*, *Esquire*,
enRoute, and *New York* magazine. He lives in Toronto
with his wife, Carol, and son, Cormac.

CLARKSON POTTER/PUBLISHERS
NEW YORK
CLARKSONPOTTER.COM

COVER DESIGN: ROBERT DIAZ
COVER PHOTOGRAPHS: MAYA VISNYEI
ENDPAPER ILLUSTRATIONS: CLAIRE MCCRACKEN